D1518521

THE VOICE OF THE CITY.

" *The Voice of the City.*"

THE VOICE OF THE CITY

FURTHER STORIES OF THE FOUR MILLION

BY

O. HENRY

Author of "The Four Million," "The Trimmed Lamp," "Strictly Business," "Whirligigs," "Sixes and Sevens," Etc.

PUBLISHED BY
DOUBLEDAY, PAGE & COMPANY
FOR
REVIEW OF REVIEWS CO.
1913

Acknowledgment is made to the New York *World* and to *Ainslee's Magazine* for permission to republish these stories

CONTENTS

THE VOICE OF THE CITY

THE VOICE OF THE CITY

TWENTY-FIVE years ago the school children used to chant their lessons. The manner of their delivery was a singsong recitative between the utterance of an Episcopal minister and the drone of a tired sawmill. I mean no disrespect. We must have lumber and sawdust.

I remember one beautiful and instructive little lyric that emanated from the physiology class. The most striking line of it was this:

" The shin-bone is the long-est bone in the hu-man bod-y."

What an inestimable boon it would have been if all the corporeal and spiritual facts pertaining to man had thus been tunefully and logically inculcated in our youthful minds! But what we gained in anatomy, music and philosophy was meagre.

The other day I became confused. I needed a ray of light. I turned back to those school days for aid. But in all the nasal harmonies we whined forth from those hard benches I could not recall one that treated of the voice of agglomerated mankind.

In other words, of the composite vocal message of massed humanity.

In other words, of the Voice of a Big City.

Now, the individual voice is not lacking. We can understand the song of the poet, the ripple of the brook, the meaning of the man who wants $5 until next Monday, the inscriptions on the tombs of the Pharaohs, the language of flowers, the " step lively " of the conductor, and the prelude of the milk cans at 4 A. M. Certain large-eared ones even assert that they are wise to the vibrations of the tympanum produced by concussion of the air emanating from Mr. H. James. But who can comprehend the meaning of the voice of the city?

I went out for to see.

First, I asked Aurelia. She wore white Swiss and a hat with flowers on it, and ribbons and ends of things fluttered here and there.

" Tell me," I said, stammeringly, for I have no voice of my own, " what does this big — er — enormous — er — whopping city say? It must have a voice of some kind. Does it ever speak to you? How do you interpret its meaning? It is a tremendous mass, but it must have a key."

" Like a Saratoga trunk? " asked Aurelia.

" No," said I. " Please do not refer to the lid. I have a fancy that every city has a voice. Each one has something to say to the one who can hear it. What does the big one say to you? "

" All cities," said Aurelia, judicially, " say the

same thing. When they get through saying it there is an echo from Philadelphia. So, they are unanimous."

" Here are 4,000,000 people," said I, scholastically, " compressed upon an island, which is mostly lamb surrounded by Wall Street water. The conjunction of so many units into so small a space must result in an identity — or, or rather a homogeneity — that finds its oral expression through a common channel. It is, as you might say, a consensus of translation, concentrating in a crystallized, general idea which reveals itself in what may be termed the Voice of the City. Can you tell me what it is? "

Aurelia smiled wonderfully. She sat on the high stoop. A spray of insolent ivy bobbed against her right ear. A ray of impudent moonlight flickered upon her nose. But I was adamant, nickel-plated.

" I must go and find out," I said, " what is the Voice of this city. Other cities have voices. It is an assignment. I must have it. New York," I continued, in a rising tone, " had better not hand me a cigar and say: ' Old man, I can't talk for publication.' No other city acts in that way. Chicago says, unhesitatingly, ' I will; ' Philadelphia says, ' I should; ' New Orleans says, ' I used to; ' Louisville says, ' Don't care if I do; ' St. Louis says, ' Excuse me; ' Pittsburg says, ' Smoke up.' Now, New York ——"

Aurelia smiled.

" Very well," said I, " I must go elsewhere and find out."

I went into a palace, tile-floored, cherub-ceilinged and square with the cop. I put my foot on the brass rail and said to Billy Magnus, the best bartender in the diocese:

" Billy, you've lived in New York a long time — what kind of a song-and-dance does this old town give you? What I mean is, doesn't the gab of it seem to kind of bunch up and slide over the bar to you in a sort of amalgamated tip that hits off the burg in a kind of an epigram with a dash of bitters and a slice of —— "

" Excuse me a minute," said Billy, " somebody's punching the button at the side door."

He went away; came back with an empty tin bucket; again vanished with it full; returned and said to me:

" That was Mame. She rings twice. She likes a glass of beer for supper. Her and the kid. If you ever saw that little skeesicks of mine brace up in his high chair and take his beer and —— But, say, what was yours? I get kind of excited when I hear them two rings — was it the baseball score or gin fizz you asked for? "

" Ginger ale," I answered.

I walked up to Broadway. I saw a cop on the corner. The cops take kids up, women across, and men in. I went up to him.

"If I'm not exceeding the spiel limit," I said, "let me ask you. You see New York during its vocative hours. It is the function of you and your brother cops to preserve the acoustics of the city. There must be a civic voice that is intelligible to you. At night during your lonely rounds you must have heard it. What is the epitome of its turmoil and shouting? What does the city say to you?"

"Friend," said the policeman, spinning his club, "it don't say nothing. I get my orders from the man higher up. Say, I guess you're all right. Stand here for a few minutes and keep an eye open for the roundsman."

The cop melted into the darkness of the side street. In ten minutes he had returned.

"Married last Tuesday," he said, half gruffly. "You know how they are. She comes to that corner at nine every night for a — comes to say 'hello!' I generally manage to be there. Say, what was it you asked me a bit ago — what's doing in the city? Oh, there's a roof-garden or two just opened, twelve blocks up."

I crossed a crow's-foot of street-car tracks, and skirted the edge of an umbrageous park. An artificial Diana, gilded, heroic, poised, wind-ruled, on the tower, shimmered in the clear light of her namesake in the sky. Along came my poet, hurrying, hatted, haired, emitting dactyls, spondees and dactylis. I seized him.

" Bill," said I (in the magazine he is Cleon), " give me a lift. I am on an assignment to find out the Voice of the city. You see, it's a special order. Ordinarily a symposium comprising the views of Henry Clews, John L. Sullivan, Edwin Markham, May Irwin and Charles Schwab would be about all. But this is a different matter. We want a broad, poetic, mystic vocalization of the city's soul and meaning. You are the very chap to give me a hint. Some years ago a man got at the Niagara Falls and gave us its pitch. The note was about two feet below the lowest G on the piano. Now, you can't put New York into a note unless it's better indorsed than that. But give me an idea of what it would say if it should speak. It is bound to be a mighty and far-reaching utterance. To arrive at it we must take the tremendous crash of the chords of the day's traffic, the laughter and music of the night, the solemn tones of Dr. Parkhurst, the rag-time, the weeping, the stealthy hum of cab-wheels, the shout of the press agent, the tinkle of fountains on the roof gardens, the hullabaloo of the strawberry vender and the covers of *Everybody's Magazine*, the whispers of the lovers in the parks — all these sounds must go into your Voice — not combined, but mixed, and of the mixture an essence made; and of the essence an extract — an audible extract, of which one drop shall form the thing we seek."

"Do you remember," asked the poet, with a chuckle, "that California girl we met at Stiver's studio last week? Well, I'm on my way to see her. She repeated that poem of mine, ' The Tribute of Spring,' word for word. She's the smartest proposition in this town just at present. Say, how does this confounded tie look? I spoiled four before I got one to set right."

"And the Voice that I asked you about?" I inquired.

"Oh, she doesn't sing," said Cleon. "But you ought to hear her recite my ' Angel of the Inshore Wind.' "

I passed on. I cornered a newsboy and he flashed at me prophetic pink papers that outstripped the news by two revolutions of the clock's longest hand.

"Son," I said, while I pretended to chase coins in my penny pocket, " doesn't it sometimes seem to you as if the city ought to be able to talk? All these ups and downs and funny business and queer things happening every day — what would it say, do you think, if it could speak? "

"Quit yer kiddin'," said the boy. "Wot paper yer want? I got no time to waste. It's Mag's birthday, and I want thirty cents to git her a present."

Here was no interpreter of the city's mouthpiece.

I bought a paper, and consigned its undeclared treaties, its premeditated murders and unfought battles to an ash can.

Again I repaired to the park and sat in the moon shade. I thought and thought, and wondered why none could tell me what I asked for.

And then, as swift as light from a fixed star, the answer came to me. I arose and hurried — hurried as so many reasoners must, back around my circle. I knew the answer and I hugged it in my breast as I flew, fearing lest some one would stop me and demand my secret.

Aurelia was still on the stoop. The moon was higher and the ivy shadows were deeper. I sat at her side and we watched a little cloud tilt at the drifting moon and go asunder, quite pale and discomfited.

And then, wonder of wonders and delight of delights! our hands somehow touched, and our fingers closed together and did not part.

After half an hour Aurelia said, with that smile of hers:

" Do you know, you haven't spoken a word since you came back ! "

" That," said I, nodding wisely, " is the Voice of the City."

THE COMPLETE LIFE OF JOHN HOPKINS

THERE is a saying that no man has tasted the full flavor of life until he has known poverty, love and war. The justness of this reflection commends it to the lover of condensed philosophy. The three conditions embrace about all there is in life worth knowing. A surface thinker might deem that wealth should be added to the list. Not so. When a poor man finds a long-hidden quarter-dollar that has slipped through a rip into his vest lining, he sounds the pleasure of life with a deeper plummet than any millionaire can hope to cast.

It seems that the wise executive power that rules life has thought best to drill man in these three conditions; and none may escape all three. In rural places the terms do not mean so much. Poverty is less pinching; love is temperate; war shrinks to contests about boundary lines and the neighbors' hens. It is in the cities that our epigram gains in truth and vigor; and it has remained for one John Hopkins to crowd the experience into a rather small space of time.

The Hopkins flat was like a thousand others. There was a rubber plant in one window; a flea-bitten terrier sat in the other, wondering when he was to have his day.

John Hopkins was like a thousand others. He worked at $20 per week in a nine-story, red-brick building at either Insurance, Buckle's Hoisting Engines, Chiropody, Loans, Pulleys, Boas Renovated, Waltz Guaranteed in Five Lessons, or Artificial Limbs. It is not for us to wring Mr. Hopkins's avocation from these outward signs that be.

Mrs. Hopkins was like a thousand others. The auriferous tooth, the sedentary disposition, the Sunday afternoon wanderlust, the draught upon the delicatessen store for home-made comforts, the furor for department store marked-down sales, the feeling of superiority to the lady in the third-floor front who wore genuine ostrich tips and had two names over her bell, the mucilaginous hours during which she remained glued to the window sill, the vigilant avoidance of the instalment man, the tireless patronage of the acoustics of the dumb-waiter shaft — all the attributes of the Gotham flat-dweller were hers.

One moment yet of sententiousness and the story moves.

In the Big City large and sudden things happen. You round a corner and thrust the rib of your umbrella into the eye of your old friend from Kootenai Falls. You stroll out to pluck a Sweet William in the park — and lo! bandits attack you — you are ambulanced to the hospital — you marry your nurse; are divorced — get squeezed while short on U. P. S. and D. O. W. N. S.— stand in the bread line — marry an heiress, take out your laundry and pay your club dues — seemingly all in the wink of an eye. You travel the streets, and a finger beckons to you, a handkerchief is dropped for you, a brick is dropped upon you, the elevator cable or your bank breaks, a table d'hôte or your wife disagrees with you, and Fate tosses you about like cork crumbs in wine opened by an un-feed waiter. The City is a sprightly youngster, and you are red paint upon its toy, and you get licked off.

John Hopkins sat, after a compressed dinner, in his glove-fitting straight-front flat. He sat upon a hornblende couch and gazed, with satiated eyes, at Art Brought Home to the People in the shape of " The Storm " tacked against the wall. Mrs. Hopkins discoursed droningly of the dinner smells from the flat across the hall. The flea-bitten terrier gave Hopkins a look of disgust, and showed a man-hating tooth.

Here was neither poverty, love, nor war; but upon such barren stems may be grafted those essentials of a complete life.

John Hopkins sought to inject a few raisins of conversation into the tasteless dough of existence.

" Putting a new elevator in at the office," he said, discarding the nominative noun, " and the boss has turned out his whiskers."

" You don't mean it ! " commented Mrs. Hopkins.

" Mr. Whipples," continued John, " wore his new spring suit down to-day. I liked it fine. It's a gray with ——" He stopped, suddenly stricken by a need that made itself known to him. " I believe I'll walk down to the corner and get a five-cent cigar," he concluded.

John Hopkins took his hat and picked his way down the musty halls and stairs of the flat-house.

The evening air was mild, and the streets shrill with the careless cries of children playing games controlled by mysterious rhythms and phrases. Their elders held the doorways and steps with leisurely pipe and gossip. Paradoxically, the fire-escapes supported lovers in couples who made no attempt to fly the mounting conflagration they were there to fan.

The corner cigar store aimed at by John Hopkins was kept by a man named Freshmayer, who looked upon the earth as a sterile promontory.

Hopkins, unknown in the store, entered and called genially for his " bunch of spinach, car-fare grade." This imputation deepened the pessimism of Freshmayer; but he set out a brand that came perilously near to filling the order. Hopkins bit off the roots of his purchase, and lighted up at the swinging gas jet. Feeling in his pockets to make payment, he found not a penny there.

" Say, my friend," he explained, frankly, " I've come out without any change. Hand you that nickel first time I pass."

Joy surged in Freshmayer's heart. Here was corroboration of his belief that the world was rotten and man a peripatetic evil. Without a word he rounded the end of his counter and made earnest onslaught upon his customer. Hopkins was no man to serve as a punching-bag for a pessimistic tobacconist. He quickly bestowed upon Freshmayer a colorado-maduro eye in return for the ardent kick that he received from that dealer in goods for cash only.

The impetus of the enemy's attack forced the Hopkins line back to the sidewalk. There the conflict raged; the pacific wooden Indian, with his carven smile, was overturned, and those of the street who delighted in carnage pressed round to view the zealous joust.

But then came the inevitable cop and imminent inconvenience for both the attacker and attacked. John Hopkins was a peaceful citizen, who worked at rebuses of nights in a flat, but he was not without the fundamental spirit of resistance that comes with the battle-rage. He knocked the policeman into a grocer's sidewalk display of goods and gave Freshmayer a punch that caused him temporarily to regret that

he had not made it a rule to extend a five-cent line
of credit to certain customers. Then Hopkins took
spiritedly to his heels down the sidewalk, closely followed by the cigar-dealer and the policeman, whose
uniform testified to the reason in the grocer's sign
that read: "Eggs cheaper than anywhere else in
the city."

As Hopkins ran he became aware of a big, low,
red, racing automobile that kept abreast of him in
the street. This auto steered in to the side of the
sidewalk, and the man guiding it motioned to Hopkins
to jump into it. He did so without slackening his
speed, and fell into the turkey-red upholstered seat
beside the chauffeur. The big machine, with a dimin-
uendo cough, flew away like an albatross down the
avenue into which the street emptied.

The driver of the auto sped his machine without a
word. He was masked beyond guess in the goggles
and diabolic garb of the chauffeur.

"Much obliged, old man," called Hopkins, gratefully. "I guess you've got sporting blood in you,
all right, and don't admire the sight of two men
trying to soak one. Little more and I'd have been
pinched."

The chauffeur made no sign that he had heard.
Hopkins shrugged a shoulder and chewed at his
cigar, to which his teeth had clung grimly through-
out the mêlée.

Ten minutes and the auto turned into the open carriage entrance of a noble mansion of brown stone, and stood still. The chauffeur leaped out, and said:

" Come quick. The lady, she will explain. It is the great honor you will have, monsieur. Ah, that milady could call upon Armand to do this thing! But, no, I am only one chauffeur."

With vehement gestures the chauffeur conducted Hopkins into the house. He was ushered into a small but luxurious reception chamber. A lady, young, and possessing the beauty of visions, rose from a chair. In her eyes smouldered a becoming anger. Her high-arched, thread-like brows were ruffled into a delicious frown.

" Milady," said the chauffeur, bowing low, " I have the honor to relate to you that I went to the house of Monsieur Long and found him to be not at home. As I came back I see this gentleman in combat against — how you say — greatest odds. He is fighting with five — ten — thirty men — gendarmes, *aussi.* Yes, milady, he what you call ' swat ' one — three — eight policemans. If that Monsieur Long is out I say to myself this gentleman he will serve milady so well, and I bring him here."

" Very well, Armand," said the lady, " you may go." She turned to Hopkins.

" I sent my chauffeur," she said, " to bring my cousin, Walter Long. There is a man in this house who has treated me with insult and abuse. I have complained to my aunt, and she laughs at me. Armand says you are brave. In these prosaic days men who are both brave and chivalrous are few. May I count upon your assistance?"

John Hopkins thrust the remains of his cigar into his coat pocket. He looked upon this winning creature and felt his first thrill of romance. It was a knightly love, and contained no disloyalty to the flat with the flea-bitten terrier and the lady of his choice. He had married her after a picnic of the Lady Label Stickers' Union, Lodge No. 2, on a dare and a bet of new hats and chowder all around with his friend, Billy McManus. This angel who was begging him to come to her rescue was something too heavenly for chowder, and as for hats — golden, jewelled crowns for her!

"Say," said John Hopkins, "just show me the guy that you've got the grouch at. I've neglected my talents as a scrapper heretofore, but this is my busy night."

"He is in there," said the lady, pointing to a closed door. "Come. Are you sure that you do not falter or fear?"

"Me?" said John Hopkins. "Just give me one of those roses in the bunch you are wearing, will you?"

The lady gave him a red, red rose. John Hopkins kissed it, stuffed it into his vest pocket, opened the door and walked into the room. It was a handsome library, softly but brightly lighted. A young man was there, reading.

" Books on etiquette is what you want to study," said John Hopkins, abruptly. " Get up here, and I'll give you some lessons. Be rude to a lady, will you? "

The young man looked mildly surprised. Then he arose languidly, dextrously caught the arms of John Hopkins and conducted him irresistibly to the front door of the house.

" Beware, Ralph Branscombe," cried the lady, who had followed, " what you do to the gallant man who has tried to protect me."

The young man shoved John Hopkins gently out the door and then closed it.

" Bess," he said calmly, " I wish you would quit reading historical novels. How in the world did that fellow get in here? "

" Armand brought him," said the young lady. " I think you are awfully mean not to let me have that St. Bernard. I sent Armand for Walter. I was so angry with you."

" Be sensible, Bess," said the young man, taking her arm. " That dog isn't safe. He has bitten two or three people around the kennels. Come now, let's go tell auntie we are in good humor again."

Arm in arm, they moved away.

John Hopkins walked to his flat. The janitor's

five-year-old daughter was playing on the steps.
Hopkins gave her a nice, red rose and walked upstairs.

Mrs. Hopkins was philandering with curl-papers.
" Get your cigar? " she asked, disinterestedly.

" Sure," said Hopkins, " and I knocked around a
while outside.   It's a nice night."

He sat upon the hornblende sofa, took out the
stump of his cigar, lighted it, and gazed at the graceful figures in " The Storm " on the opposite wall.

" I was telling you," said he, " about Mr.
Whipple's suit.   It's a gray, with an invisible check,
and it looks fine."

A LICKPENNY LOVER

THERE were 3,000 girls in the Biggest Store. Masie was one of them. She was eighteen and a saleslady in the gents' gloves. Here she became versed in two varieties of human beings — the kind of gents who buy their gloves in department stores and the kind of women who buy gloves for unfortunate gents. Besides this wide knowledge of the human species, Masie had acquired other information. She had listened to the promulgated wisdom of the 2,999 other girls and had stored it in a brain that was as secretive and wary as that of a Maltese cat. Perhaps nature, foreseeing that she would lack wise counsellors, had mingled the saving ingredient of shrewdness along with her beauty, as she has endowed the silver fox of the priceless fur above the other animals with cunning.

For Masie was beautiful. She was a deep-tinted blonde, with the calm poise of a lady who cooks butter cakes in a window. She stood behind her counter in the Biggest Store; and as you closed your hand over the tape-line for your glove measure you thought of Hebe; and as you looked again you wondered how she had come by Minerva's eyes.

21

When the floorwalker was not looking Masie chewed tutti frutti; when he was looking she gazed up as if at the clouds and smiled wistfully.

That is the shopgirl smile, and I enjoin you to shun it unless you are well fortified with callosity of the heart, caramels and a congeniality for the capers of Cupid. This smile belonged to Masie's recreation hours and not to the store; but the floorwalker must have his own. He is the Shylock of the stores. When he comes nosing around the bridge of his nose is a toll-bridge. It is goo-goo eyes or " git " when he looks toward a pretty girl. Of course not all floorwalkers are thus. Only a few days ago the papers printed news of one over eighty years of age.

One day Irving Carter, painter, millionaire, traveller, poet, automobilist, happened to enter the Biggest Store. It is due to him to add that his visit was not voluntary. Filial duty took him by the collar and dragged him inside, while his mother philandered among the bronze and terra-cotta statuettes.

Carter strolled across to the glove counter in order to shoot a few minutes on the wing. His need for gloves was genuine; he had forgotten to bring a pair with him. But his action hardly calls for apology, because he had never heard of glove-counter flirtations.

As he neared the vicinity of his fate he hesitated, suddenly conscious of this unknown phase of Cupid's less worthy profession.

Three or four cheap fellows, sonorously garbed, were leaning over the counters, wrestling with the mediatorial hand-coverings, while giggling girls played vivacious seconds to their lead upon the strident string of coquetry. Carter would have retreated, but he had gone too far. Masie confronted him behind her counter with a questioning look in eyes as coldly, beautifully, warmly blue as the glint of summer sunshine on an iceberg drifting in Southern seas.

And then Irving Carter, painter, millionaire, etc., felt a warm flush rise to his aristocratically pale face. But not from diffidence. The blush was intellectual in origin. He knew in a moment that he stood in the ranks of the ready-made youths who wooed the giggling girls at other counters. Himself leaned against the oaken trysting place of a cockney Cupid with a desire in his heart for the favor of a glove salesgirl. He was no more than Bill and Jack and Mickey. And then he felt a sudden tolerance for them, and an elating, courageous contempt for the conventions upon which he had fed, and an unhesitating determination to have this perfect creature for his own.

When the gloves were paid for and wrapped Carter lingered for a moment. The dimples at the corners of Masie's damask mouth deepened. All gentlemen who bought gloves lingered in just that way. She curved an arm, showing like Psyche's through her shirt-waist sleeve, and rested an elbow upon the show-case edge.

Carter had never before encountered a situation of which he had not been perfect master. But now he stood far more awkward than Bill or Jack or Mickey. He had no chance of meeting this beautiful girl socially. His mind struggled to recall the nature and habits of shopgirls as he had read or heard of them. Somehow he had received the idea that they sometimes did not insist too strictly upon the regular channels of introduction. His heart beat loudly at the thought of proposing an unconventional meeting with this lovely and virginal being. But the tumult in his heart gave him courage.

After a few friendly and well-received remarks on general subjects, he laid his card by her hand on the counter.

" Will you please pardon me," he said, " if I seem too bold; but I earnestly hope you will allow me the pleasure of seeing you again. There is my name; I assure you that it is with the greatest respect that I ask the favor of becoming one of your fr —— acquaintances. May I not hope for the privilege? "

Masie knew men — especially men who buy gloves. Without hesitation she looked him frankly and smilingly in the eyes, and said:

" Sure. I guess you're all right. I don't usually go out with strange gentlemen, though. It ain't quite ladylike. When should you want to see me again?"

"As soon as I may," said Carter. "If you would allow me to call at your home, I ——"

Masie laughed musically. "Oh, gee, no!" she said, emphatically. "If you could see our flat once! There's five of us in three rooms. I'd just like to see ma's face if I was to bring a gentleman friend there!"

"Anywhere, then," said the enamored Carter, "that will be convenient to you."

"Say," suggested Masie, with a bright-idea look in her peach-blow face; "I guess Thursday night will about suit me. Suppose you come to the corner of Eighth Avenue and Forty-eighth Street at 7:30. I live right near the corner. But I've got to be back home by eleven. Ma never lets me stay out after eleven."

Carter promised gratefully to keep the tryst, and then hastened to his mother, who was looking about for him to ratify her purchase of a bronze Diana.

A salesgirl, with small eyes and an obtuse nose, strolled near Masie, with a friendly leer.

"Did you make a hit with his nobs, Mase?" she asked, familiarly.

"The gentleman asked permission to call," answered Masie, with the grand air, as she slipped Carter's card into the bosom of her waist.

" Permission to call!" echoed small eyes, with a snigger. " Did he say anything about dinner in the Waldorf and a spin in his auto afterward? "

" Oh, cheese it!" said Masie, wearily. " You've been used to swell things, I don't think. You've had a swelled head ever since that hose-cart driver took you out to a chop suey joint. No, he never mentioned the Waldorf; but there's a Fifth Avenue address on his card, and if he buys the supper you can bet your life there won't be no pigtail on the waiter what takes the order."

As Carter glided away from the Biggest Store with his mother in his electric runabout, he bit his lip with a dull pain at his heart. He knew that love had come to him for the first time in all the twenty-nine years of his life. And that the object of it should make so readily an appointment with him at a street corner, though it was a step toward his desires, tortured him with misgivings.

Carter did not know the shopgirl. He did not know that her home is often either a scarcely habitable tiny room or a domicile filled to overflowing with kith and kin. The street-corner is her parlor, the park is her drawing-room; the avenue is her garden walk; yet for the most part she is as inviolate mistress of herself in them as is my lady inside her tapestried chamber.

One evening at dusk, two weeks after their first

meeting, Carter and Masie strolled arm-in-arm into a little, dimly-lit park. They found a bench, tree-shadowed and secluded, and sat there.

For the first time his arm stole gently around her. Her golden-bronze head slid restfully against his shoulder.

" Gee ! " sighed Masie, thankfully. " Why didn't you ever think of that before? "

" Masie," said Carter, earnestly, " you surely know that I love you. I ask you sincerely to marry me. You know me well enough by this time to have no doubts of me. I want you, and I must have you. I care nothing for the difference in our stations."

" What is the difference? " asked Masie, curiously.

" Well, there isn't any," said Carter, quickly, " except in the minds of foolish people. It is in my power to give you a life of luxury. My social position is beyond dispute, and my means are ample."

" They all say that," remarked Masie. " It's the kid they all give you. I suppose you really work in a delicatessen or follow the races. I ain't as green as I look."

" I can furnish you all the proofs you want," said Carter, gently. " And I want you, Masie. I loved you the first day I saw you."

" They all do," said Masie, with an amused laugh, " to hear 'em talk. If I could meet a man that got stuck on me the third time he'd seen me I think I'd get mashed on him."

" Please don't say such things," pleaded Carter. " Listen to me, dear. Ever since I first looked into your eyes you have been the only woman in the world for me."

" Oh, ain't you the kidder! " smiled Masie. " How many other girls did you ever tell that? "

But Carter persisted. And at length he reached the flimsy, fluttering little soul of the shopgirl that existed somewhere deep down in her lovely bosom. His words penetrated the heart whose very lightness was its safest armor. She looked up at him with eyes that saw. And a warm glow visited her cool cheeks. Tremblingly, awfully, her moth wings closed, and she seemed about to settle upon the flower of love. Some faint glimmer of life and its possibilities on the other side of her glove counter dawned upon her. Carter felt the change and crowded the opportunity.

" Marry me, Masie," he whispered softly, " and we will go away from this ugly city to beautiful ones. We will forget work and business, and life will be one long holiday. I know where I should take you — I have been there often. Just think of a shore where summer is eternal, where the waves are always rippling on the lovely beach and the people are happy and free as children. We will sail to those shores and remain there as long as you please. In one of those

far-away cities there are grand and lovely palaces
and towers full of beautiful pictures and statues.
The streets of the city are water, and one travels
about in ——"

"I know," said Masie, sitting up suddenly.
"Gondolas."

"Yes," smiled Carter.

"I thought so," said Masie.

"And then," continued Carter, "we will travel on
and see whatever we wish in the world. After the
European cities we will visit India and the ancient
cities there, and ride on elephants and see the wonderful temples of the Hindoos and Brahmins and the
Japanese gardens and the camel trains and chariot
races in Persia, and all the queer sights of foreign
countries. Don't you think you would like it, Masie?"

Masie rose to her feet.

"I think we had better be going home," she said,
coolly. "It's getting late."

Carter humored her. He had come to know her
varying, thistle-down moods, and that it was useless
to combat them. But he felt a certain happy triumph.
He had held for a moment, though but by a silken
thread, the soul of his wild Psyche, and hope was
stronger within him. Once she had folded her wings
and her cool hand had closed about his own.

At the Biggest Store the next day Masie's chum,
Lulu, waylaid her in an angle of the counter.

" How are you and your swell friend making it? "
she asked.

" Oh, him? " said Masie, patting her side curls.
" He ain't in it any more. Say, Lu, what do you
think that fellow wanted me to do? "

" Go on the stage? " guessed Lulu, breathlessly.

" Nit; he's too cheap a guy for that. He wanted
me to marry him and go down to Coney Island for
a wedding tour! "

DOUGHERTY'S EYE-OPENER

BIG JIM DOUGHERTY was a sport. He belonged to that race of men. In Manhattan it is a distinct race. They are the Caribs of the North — strong, artful, self-sufficient, clannish, honorable within the laws of their race, holding in lenient contempt neighboring tribes who bow to the measure of Society's tapeline. I refer, of course, to the titled nobility of sportdom. There is a class which bears as a qualifying adjective the substantive belonging to a wind instrument made of a cheap and base metal. But the tin mines of Cornwall never produced the material for manufacturing descriptive nomenclature for " Big Jim " Dougherty.

The habitat of the sport is the lobby or the outside corner of certain hotels and combination restaurants and cafés. They are mostly men of different sizes, running from small to large; but they are unanimous in the possession of a recently shaven, blue-black cheek and chin and dark overcoats (in season) with black velvet collars.

Of the domestic life of the sport little is known. It has been said that Cupid and Hymen sometimes take a hand in the game and copper the queen of hearts to lose. Daring theorists have averred — not content with simply saying — that a sport often contracts a spouse, and even incurs descendants. Sometimes he sits in the game of politics; and then at chowder picnics there is a revelation of a Mrs. Sport and little Sports in glazed hats with tin pails.

But mostly the sport is Oriental. He believes his women-folk should not be too patent. Somewhere behind grilles or flower-ornamented fire escapes they await him. There, no doubt, they tread on rugs from Teheran and are diverted by the bulbul and play upon the dulcimer and feed upon sweetmeats. But away from his home the sport is an integer. He does not, as men of other races in Manhattan do, become the convoy in his unoccupied hours of fluttering laces and high heels that tick off delectably the happy seconds of the evening parade. He herds with his own race at corners, and delivers a commentary in his Carib lingo upon the passing show.

"Big Jim" Dougherty had a wife, but he did not wear a button portrait of her upon his lapel. He had a home in one of those brown-stone, iron-railed streets on the west side that look like a recently excavated bowling alley of Pompeii.

To this home of his Mr. Dougherty repaired each night when the hour was so late as to promise no further diversion in the arch domains of sport. By that time the occupant of the monogamistic harem would be in dreamland, the bulbul silenced and the hour propitious for slumber.

" Big Jim " always arose at twelve, meridian, for breakfast, and soon afterward he would return to the rendezvous of his " crowd."

He was always vaguely conscious that there was a Mrs. Dougherty. He would have received without denial the charge that the quiet, neat, comfortable little woman across the table at home was his wife. In fact, he remembered pretty well that they had been married for nearly four years. She would often tell him about the cute tricks of Spot, the canary, and the light-haired lady that lived in the window of the flat across the street.

" Big Jim " Dougherty even listened to this conversation of hers sometimes. He knew that she would have a nice dinner ready for him every evening at seven when he came for it. She sometimes went to matinées, and she had a talking machine with six dozen records. Once when her Uncle Amos blew in on a wind from up-state, she went with him to the Eden Musée. Surely these things were diversions enough for any woman.

One afternoon Mr. Dougherty finished his breakfast, put on his hat and got away fairly for the door. When his hand was on the knob he heard his wife's voice.

" Jim," she said, firmly, " I wish you would take

me out to dinner this evening. It has been three years since you have been outside the door with me."

"Big Jim" was astounded. She had never asked anything like this before. It had the flavor of a totally new proposition. But he was a game sport.

"All right," he said. "You be ready when I come at seven. None of this ' wait two minutes till I primp an hour or two ' kind of business, now, Dele."

"I'll be ready," said his wife, calmly.

At seven she descended the stone steps in the Pompeian bowling alley at the side of " Big Jim " Dougherty. She wore a dinner gown made of a stuff that the spiders must have woven, and of a color that a twilight sky must have contributed. A light coat with many admirably unnecessary capes and adorably inutile ribbons floated downward from her shoulders. Fine feathers do make fine birds; and the only reproach in the saying is for the man who refuses to give up his earnings to the ostrich-tip industry.

"Big Jim " Dougherty was troubled. There was a being at his side whom he did not know. He thought of the sober-hued plumage that this bird of paradise was accustomed to wear in her cage, and this winged revelation puzzled him. In some way she reminded him of the Delia Cullen that he had married four years before. Shyly and rather awkwardly he stalked at her right hand.

"After dinner I'll take you back home, Dele," said

Mr. Dougherty, " and then I'll drop back up to Seltzer's with the boys. You can have swell chuck to-
night if you want it. I made a winning on Anaconda
yesterday; so you can go as far as you like."

Mr. Dougherty had intended to make the outing
with his unwonted wife an inconspicuous one. Uxori-
ousness was a weakness that the precepts of the
Caribs did not countenance. If any of his friends of
the track, the billiard cloth or the square circle had
wives they had never complained of the fact in public.
There were a number of table d'hôte places on the
cross streets near the broad and shining way; and to
one of these he had purposed to escort her, so that the
bushel might not be removed from the light of his
domesticity.

But while on the way Mr. Dougherty altered those
intentions. He had been casting stealthy glances at
his attractive companion and he was seized with the
conviction that she was no selling plater. He re-
solved to parade with his wife past Seltzer's café,
where at this time a number of his tribe would be
gathered to view the daily evening procession. Yes;
and he would take her to dine at Hoogley's, the swell-
est slow-lunch warehouse on the line, he said to
himself.

The congregation of smooth-faced tribal gentlemen were on watch at Seltzer's. As Mr. Dougherty
and his reorganized Delia passed they stared, mo-

mentarily petrified, and then removed their hats — a
performance as unusual to them as was the astonish-
ing innovation presented to their gaze by " Big Jim."
On the latter gentleman's impassive face there appeared a slight flicker of triumph — a faint flicker,
no more to be observed than the expression called
there by the draft of little casino to a four-card spade
flush.

Hoogley's was animated. Electric lights shone —
as, indeed, they were expected to do. And the napery,
the glassware and the flowers also meritoriously per-
formed the spectacular duties required of them.   The
guests were numerous, well-dressed and gay.

A waiter — not necessarily obsequious — conducted
" Big Jim " Dougherty and his wife to a table.

" Play that menu straight across for what you like,
Dele," said " Big Jim."   " It's you for a trough of
the gilded oats to-night.   It strikes me that maybe
we've been sticking too fast to home fodder."

" Big Jim's " wife gave her order.   He looked at
her with respect.   She had mentioned truffles ; and he
had not known that she knew what truffles were. From
the wine list she designated an appropriate and desirable brand. He looked at her with some admiration.

She was beaming with the innocent excitement that
woman derives from the exercise of her gregarious-
ness.   She was talking to him about a hundred things
with animation and delight.   And as the meal pro-

gressed her cheeks, colorless from a life indoors, took on a delicate flush. "Big Jim" looked around the room and saw that none of the women there had her charm. And then he thought of the three years she had suffered immurement, uncomplaining, and a flush of shame warmed him, for he carried fair play as an item in his creed.

But when the Honorable Patrick Corrigan, leader in Dougherty's district and a friend of his, saw them and came over to the table, matters got to the three-quarter stretch. The Honorable Patrick was a gallant man, both in deeds and words. As for the Blarney stone, his previous actions toward it must have been pronounced. Heavy damages for breach of promise could surely have been obtained had the Blarney stone seen fit to sue the Honorable Patrick.

"Jimmy, old man!" he called; he clapped Dougherty on the back; he shone like a midday sun upon Delia.

"Honorable Mr. Corrigan — Mrs. Dougherty," said "Big Jim."

The Honorable Patrick became a fountain of entertainment and admiration. The waiter had to fetch a third chair for him; he made another at the table, and the wineglasses were refilled.

"You selfish old rascal!" he exclaimed, shaking an arch finger at "Big Jim," "to have kept Mrs. Dougherty a secret from us."

And then " Big Jim " Dougherty, who was no
talker, sat dumb, and saw the wife who had dined
every evening for three years at home, blossom like
a fairy flower. Quick, witty, charming, full of light
and ready talk, she received the experienced attack
of the Honorable Patrick on the field of repartee and
surprised, vanquished, delighted him. She unfolded
her long-closed petals and around her the room
became a garden. They tried to include " Big
Jim " in the conversation, but he was without a
vocabulary.

And then a stray bunch of politicians and good
fellows who lived for sport came into the room. They
saw " Big Jim " and the leader, and over they came
and were made acquainted with Mrs. Dougherty. And
in a few minutes she was holding a salon. Half a
dozen men surrounded her, courtiers all, and six
found her capable of charming. " Big Jim " sat,
grim, and kept saying to himself: " Three years,
three years ! "

The dinner came to an end. The Honorable Patrick reached for Mrs. Dougherty's cloak; but that
was a matter of action instead of words, and Dougherty's big hand got it first by two seconds.

While the farewells were being said at the door
the Honorable Patrick smote Dougherty mightily
between the shoulders.

" Jimmy, me boy," he declared, in a giant whisper, " the madam is a jewel of the first water. Ye're a lucky dog."

"Big Jim" walked homeward with his wife. She seemed quite as pleased with the lights and show windows in the streets as with the admiration of the men in Hoogley's. As they passed Seltzer's they heard the sound of many voices in the café. The boys would be starting the drinks around now and discussing past performances.

At the door of their home Delia paused. The pleasure of the outing radiated softly from her countenance. She could not hope for Jim of evenings, but the glory of this one would lighten her lonely hours for a long time.

"Thank you for taking me out, Jim," she said, gratefully. "You'll be going back up to Seltzer's now, of course."

"To —— with Seltzer's," said "Big Jim," em-emphatically. "And d—— Pat Corrigan! Does he think I haven't got any eyes?"

And the door closed behind both of them.

"LITTLE SPECK IN GARNERED FRUIT"

THE honeymoon was at its full. There was a flat with the reddest of new carpets, tasselled portières and six steins with pewter lids arranged on a ledge above the wainscoting of the dining-room. The wonder of it was yet upon them. Neither of them had ever seen a yellow primrose by the river's brim; but if such a sight had met their eyes at that time it would have seemed like — well, whatever the poet expected the right kind of people to see in it besides a primrose.

The bride sat in the rocker with her feet resting upon the world. She was wrapt in rosy dreams and a kimono of the same hue. She wondered what the people in Greenland and Tasmania and Beloochistan were saying one to another about her marriage to Kid McGarry. Not that it made any difference. There was no welter-weight from London to the Southern Cross that could stand up four hours — no; four rounds — with her bridegroom. And he had been hers for three weeks; and the crook of her little finger could sway him more than the fist of any 142-pounder in the world.

Love, when it is ours, is the other name for self-abnegation and sacrifice. When it belongs to people across the airshaft it means arrogance and self-conceit.

The bride crossed her oxfords and looked thoughtfully at the distemper Cupids on the ceiling.

" Precious," said she, with the air of Cleopatra asking Antony for Rome done up in tissue paper and delivered at residence, " I think I would like a peach."

Kid McGarry arose and put on his coat and hat. He was serious, shaven, sentimental, and spry.

" All right," said he, as coolly as though he were only agreeing to sign articles to fight the champion of England. " I'll step down and cop one out for you — see? "

" Don't be long," said the bride. " I'll be lonesome without my naughty boy. Get a nice, ripe one."

After a series of farewells that would have befitted an imminent voyage to foreign parts, the Kid went down to the street.

Here he not unreasonably hesitated, for the season was yet early spring, and there seemed small chance of wresting anywhere from those chill streets and stores the coveted luscious guerdon of summer's golden prime.

At the Italian's fruit-stand on the corner he stopped and cast a contemptuous eye over the display of papered oranges, highly polished apples and wan, sun-hungry bananas.

" Gotta da peach? " asked the Kid in the tongue of Dante, the lover of lovers.

" Ah, no," sighed the vender. " Not for one mont com-a da peach. Too soon. Gotta da nice-a orange. Like-a da orange? "

Scornful, the Kid pursued his quest. He entered the all-night chop-house, café, and bowling-alley of his friend and admirer, Justus O'Callahan. The O'Callahan was about in his institution, looking for leaks.

" I want it straight," said the Kid to him. " The old woman has got a hunch that she wants a peach. Now, if you've got a peach, Cal, get it out quick. I want it and others like it if you've got 'em in plural quantities."

" The house is yours," said O'Callahan. " But there's no peach in it. It's too soon. I don't suppose you could even find 'em at one of the Broadway joints. That's too bad. When a lady fixes her mouth for a certain kind of fruit nothing else won't do. It's too late now to find any of the first-class fruiterers open. But if you think the missis would like some nice oranges I've just got a box of fine ones in that she might ——"

" Much obliged, Cal. It's a peach proposition right from the ring of the gong. I'll try further."

The time was nearly midnight as the Kid walked down the West-Side avenue. Few stores were open, and such as were practically hooted at the idea of a peach.

But in her moated flat the bride confidently awaited her Persian fruit.   A champion welter-weight not find a peach? — not stride triumphantly over the seasons and the zodiac and the almanac to fetch an Amsden's June or a Georgia cling to his owny-own?

The Kid's eye caught sight of a window that was lighted and gorgeous with nature's most entrancing colors.   The light suddenly went out.   The Kid sprinted and caught the fruiterer locking his door.

"Peaches?" said he, with extreme deliberation.

"Well, no, sir.   Not for three or four weeks yet. I haven't any idea where you might find some.   There may be a few in town from under the glass, but they'd be hard to locate.   Maybe at one of the more expensive hotels — some place where there's plenty of money to waste.   I've got some very fine oranges, though — from a shipload that came in to-day."

The Kid lingered on the corner for a moment, and then set out briskly toward a pair of green lights that flanked the steps of a building down a dark side street.

"Captain around anywhere?" he asked of the desk sergeant of the police station.

At that moment the captain came briskly forward from the rear.   He was in plain clothes and had a busy air.

"Hello, Kid," he said to the pugilist. "Thought you were bridal-touring?"

"Got back yesterday. I'm a solid citizen now. Think I'll take an interest in municipal doings. How would it suit you to get into Denver Dick's place to-night, Cap?"

"Past performances," said the captain, twisting his moustache. "Denver was closed up two months ago."

"Correct," said the Kid. "Rafferty chased him out of the Forty-third. He's running in your precinct now, and his game's bigger than ever. I'm down on this gambling business. I can put you against his game."

"In my precinct?" growled the captain. "Are you sure, Kid? I'll take it as a favor. Have you got the entrée? How is it to be done?"

"Hammers," said the Kid. "They haven't got any steel on the doors yet. You'll need ten men. No; they won't let me in the place. Denver has been trying to do me. He thought I tipped him off for the other raid. I didn't, though. You want to hurry. I've got to get back home. The house is only three blocks from here."

Before ten minutes had sped the captain with a dozen men stole with their guide into the hallway of a dark and virtuous-looking building in which many businesses were conducted by day.

" Third floor, rear," said the Kid, softly. " I'll lead the way."

Two axemen faced the door that he pointed out to them.

" It seems all quiet," said the captain, doubtfully. " Are you sure your tip is straight? "

" Cut away! " said the Kid. " It's on me if it ain't."

The axes crashed through the as yet unprotected door. A blaze of light from within poured through the smashed panels. The door fell, and the raiders sprang into the room with their guns handy.

The big room was furnished with the gaudy magnificence dear to Denver Dick's western ideas. Various well-patronized games were in progress. About fifty men who were in the room rushed upon the police in a grand break for personal liberty. The plain-clothes men had to do a little club-swinging. More than half the patrons escaped.

Denver Dick had graced his game with his own presence that night. He led the rush that was intended to sweep away the smaller body of raiders. But when he saw the Kid his manner became personal. Being in the heavy-weight class he cast himself joyfully upon his slighter enemy, and they rolled down a flight of stairs in each other's arms. On the landing they separated and arose, and then the Kid was able to use some of his professional tactics, which had been useless to him while in the excited clutch of a 200-pound sporting gentleman who was about to lose $20,000 worth of paraphernalia.

After vanquishing his adversary the Kid hurried upstairs and through the gambling-room into a smaller apartment connecting by an arched doorway.

Here was a long table set with choicest chinaware and silver, and lavishly furnished with food of that expensive and spectacular sort of which the devotees of sport are supposed to be fond. Here again was to be perceived the liberal and florid taste of the gentleman with the urban cognomenal prefix.

A No. 10 patent leather shoe protruded a few of its inches outside the tablecloth along the floor. The Kid seized this and plucked forth a black man in a white tie and the garb of a servitor.

"Get up!" commanded the Kid. "Are you in charge of this free lunch?"

"Yes, sah, I was. Has they done pinched us ag'in, boss?"

"Looks that way. Listen to me. Are there any peaches in this layout? If there ain't I'll have to throw up the sponge."

"There was three dozen, sah, when the game opened this evenin'; but I reckon the gentlemen done eat 'em all up. If you'd like to eat a fust-rate orange, sah, I kin find you some."

"Get busy," ordered the Kid, sternly, "and move

whatever peach crop you've got quick or there'll be
trouble. If anybody oranges me again to-night, I'll
knock his face off."

The raid on Denver Dick's high-priced and prodigal luncheon revealed one lone, last peach that had
escaped the epicurean jaws of the followers of
chance. Into the Kid's pocket it went, and that in-
defatigable forager departed immediately with his
prize. With scarcely a glance at the scene on the
sidewalk below, where the officers were loading their
prisoners into the patrol wagons, he moved homeward
with long, swift strides.

His heart was light as he went. So rode the
knights back to Camelot after perils and high deeds
done for their ladies fair. The Kid's lady had commanded him and he had obeyed. True, it was but a
peach that she had craved; but it had been no small
deed to glean a peach at midnight from that wintry
city where yet the February snows lay like iron.
She had asked for a peach; she was his bride; in his
pocket the peach was warming in his hand that held it
for fear that it might fall out and be lost.

On the way the Kid turned in at an all-night drug
store and said to the spectacled clerk:

" Say, sport, I wish you'd size up this rib of mine
and see if it's broke. I was in a little scrap and
bumped down a flight or two of stairs."

The druggist made an examination.

" It isn't broken," was his diagnosis ; " but you have a bruise there that looks like you'd fallen off the Flatiron twice."

" That's all right," said the Kid. " Let's have your clothesbrush, please."

The bride waited in the rosy glow of the pink lamp shade. The miracles were not all passed away. By breathing a desire for some slight thing — a flower, a pomegranate, a — oh, yes, a peach — she could send forth her man into the night, into the world which could not withstand him, and he would do her bidding.

And now he stood by her chair and laid the peach in her hand.

" Naughty boy ! " she said, fondly. " Did I say a peach ? I think I would much rather have had an orange."

Blest be the bride.

THE HARBINGER

LONG before the springtide is felt in the dull bosom of the yokel does the city man know that the grass-green goddess is upon her throne. He sits at his breakfast eggs and toast, begirt by stone walls, opens his morning paper and sees journalism leave vernalism at the post.

For, whereas, spring's couriers were once the evidence of our finer senses, now the Associated Press does the trick.

The warble of the first robin in Hackensack, the stirring of the maple sap in Bennington, the budding of the pussy willows along Main Street in Syracuse, the first chirp of the bluebird, the swan song of the Blue Point, the annual tornado in St. Louis, the plaint of the peach pessimist from Pompton, N. J., the regular visit of the tame wild goose with a broken leg to the pond near Bilgewater Junction, the base attempt of the Drug Trust to boost the price of quinine foiled in the House by Congressman Jinks, the first tall poplar struck by lightning and the usual stunned picknickers who had taken refuge, the first crack of the ice jam in the Allegheny River, the finding of a voilet in its mossy bed by the correspondent at Round Corners — these are the advance signs of the burgeoning season that are wired into the wise city, while the farmer sees nothing but winter upon his dreary fields.

But these be mere externals. The true harbinger is the heart. When Strephon seeks his Chloe and Mike his Maggie, then only is spring arrived and the newspaper report of the five-foot rattler killed in Squire Pettigrew's pasture confirmed.

Ere the first violet blew, Mr. Peters, Mr. Ragsdale and Mr. Kidd sat together on a bench in Union Square and conspired. Mr. Peters was the D'Artagnan of the loafers there. He was the dingiest, the laziest, the sorriest brown blot against the green background of any bench in the park. But just then he was the most important of the trio.

Mr. Peters had a wife. This had not heretofore affected his standing with Ragsy and Kidd. But to-day it invested him with a peculiar interest. His friends, having escaped matrimony, had shown a disposition to deride Mr. Peters for his venture on that troubled sea. But at last they had been forced to acknowledge that either he had been gifted with a large foresight or that he was one of Fortune's lucky sons.

For, Mrs. Peters had a dollar. A whole dollar bill, good and receivable by the Government for customs, taxes and all public dues. How to get possession of that dollar was the question up for discussion by the three musty musketeers.

" How do you know it was a dollar? " asked Ragsy, the immensity of the sum inclining him to scepticism.

" The coalman seen her have it," said Mr. Peters. " She went out and done some washing yesterday. And look what she give me for breakfast — the heel of a loaf and a cup of coffee, and her with a dollar! "

" It's fierce," said Ragsy.

" Say we go up and punch 'er and stick a towel in 'er mouth and cop the coin," suggested Kidd, viciously. " Y' ain't afraid of a woman, are you? "

" She might holler and have us pinched," demurred Ragsy. " I don't believe in slugging no woman in a houseful of people."

" Gent'men," said Mr. Peters, severely, through his russet stubble, " remember that you are speaking of my wife. A man who would lift his hand to a lady except in the way of —— "

" Maguire," said Ragsy, pointedly, " has got his bock beer sign out. If we had a dollar we could —— "

" Hush up! " said Mr. Peters, licking his lips. " We got to get that case note somehow, boys. Ain't what's a man's wife's his? Leave it to me. I'll go over to the house and get it. Wait here for me."

" I've seen 'em give up quick, and tell you where it's hid if you kick 'em in the ribs," said Kidd.

" No man would kick a woman," said Peters, virtuously. " A little choking — just a touch on the windpipe — that gets away with 'em — and no marks left. Wait for me. I'll bring back that dollar, boys."

High up in a tenement-house between Second Avenue and the river lived the Peterses in a back room so gloomy that the landlord blushed to take the rent for it. Mrs. Peters worked at sundry times, doing odd jobs of scrubbing and washing. Mr. Peters had a pure, unbroken record of five years without having earned a penny. And yet they clung together, sharing each other's hatred and misery, being creatures of habit. Of habit, the power that keeps the earth from flying to pieces; though there is some silly theory of gravitation.

Mrs. Peters reposed her 200 pounds on the safer of the two chairs and gazed stolidly out the one window at the brick wall opposite. Her eyes were red and damp. The furniture could have been carried away on a pushcart, but no pushcart man would have removed it as a gift.

The door opened to admit Mr. Peters. His foxterrier eyes expressed a wish. His wife's diagnosis located correctly the seat of it, but misread it hunger instead of thirst.

" You'll get nothing more to eat till night," she said, looking out of the window again. " Take your hound-dog's face out of the room."

Mr. Peters's eye calculated the distance between them. By taking her by surprise it might be possible to spring upon her, overthrow her, and apply the throttling tactics of which he had boasted to his waiting comrades. True, it had been only a boast; never yet had he dared to lay violent hands upon her; but with the thoughts of the delicious, cool bock or Culmbacher bracing his nerves, he was near to upsetting his own theories of the treatment due by a gentleman to a lady. But, with his loafer's love for the more artistic and less strenuous way, he chose diplomacy first, the high card in the game — the assumed attitude of success already attained.

"You have a dollar," he said, loftily, but significantly in the tone that goes with the lighting of a cigar — when the properties are at hand.

"I have," said Mrs. Peters, producing the bill from her bosom and crackling it, teasingly.

"I am offered a position in a — in a tea store," said Mr. Peters. "I am to begin work to-morrow. But it will be necessary for me to buy a pair of ——"

"You are a liar," said Mrs. Peters, reinterring the note. "No tea store, nor no A B C store, nor no junk shop would have you. I rubbed the skin off both me hands washin' jumpers and overalls to make that dollar. Do you think it come out of them suds to buy the kind you put into you? Skiddoo! Get your mind off of money."

Evidently the poses of Talleyrand were not worth one hundred cents on that dollar. But diplomacy is dexterous. The artistic temperament of Mr. Peters lifted him by the straps of his congress gaiters and set him on new ground. He called up a look of desperate melancholy to his eyes.

"Clara," he said, hollowly, "to struggle further is useless. You have always misunderstood me. Heaven knows I have striven with all my might to keep my head above the waves of misfortune, but —— "

"Cut out the rainbow of hope and that stuff about walkin' one by one through the narrow isles of Spain," said Mrs. Peters, with a sigh. "I've heard it so often. There's an ounce bottle of carbolic on the shelf behind the empty coffee can. Drink hearty."

Mr. Peters reflected. What next! The old expedients had failed. The two musty musketeers were awaiting him hard by the ruined château — that is to say, on a park bench with rickety cast-iron legs. His honor was at stake. He had engaged to storm the castle single-handed and bring back the treasure that was to furnish them wassail and solace. And all that stood between him and the coveted dollar was his wife, once a little girl whom he could — aha! — why not again? Once with soft words he could, as they say, twist her around his little finger. Why not again? Not for years had he tried it. Grim poverty and mutual hatred had killed all that. But Ragsy and Kidd were waiting for him to bring the dollar!

Mr. Peters took a surreptitiously keen look at his wife. Her formless bulk overflowed the chair. She kept her eyes fixed out the window in a strange kind of trance. Her eyes showed that she had been recently weeping.

" I wonder," said Mr. Peters to himself, " if there'd be anything in it."

The window was open upon its outlook of brick walls and drab, barren back yards. Except for the mildness of the air that entered it might have been midwinter yet in the city that turns such a frowning face to besieging spring. But spring doesn't come with the thunder of cannon. She is a sapper and a miner, and you must capitulate.

" I'll try it," said Mr. Peters to himself, making a wry face.

He went up to his wife and put his arm across her shoulders.

" Clara, darling," he said in tones that shouldn't have fooled a baby seal, " why should we have hard words? Ain't you my own tootsum wootsums? "

A black mark against you, Mr. Peters, in the sared ledger of Cupid. Charges of attempted graft are filed against you, and of forgery and utterance of two of Love's holiest of appellations.

But the miracle of spring was wrought. Into the

back room over the back alley between the black
walls had crept the Harbinger. It was ridiculous,
and yet —— Well, it is a rat trap, and you, madam
and sir and all of us, are in it.

Red and fat and crying like Niobe or Niagara,
Mrs. Peters threw her arms around her lord and
dissolved upon him. Mr. Peters would have striven
to extricate the dollar bill from its deposit vault,
but his arms were bound to his sides.

" Do you love me, James? " asked Mrs. Peters.

" Madly," said James, " but ——"

" You are ill! " exclaimed Mrs. Peters. " Why
are you so pale and tired looking? "

" I feel weak," said Mr. Peters. " I ——"

" Oh, wait; I know what it is. Wait, James. I'll
be back in a minute."

With a parting hug that revived in Mr. Peters
recollections of the Terrible Turk, his wife hurried
out of the room and down the stairs.

Mr. Peters hitched his thumbs under his sus-
penders.

" All right," he confided to the ceiling. " I've got
her going. I hadn't any idea the old girl was soft
any more under the foolish rib. Well, sir; ain't I
the Claude Melnotte of the lower East Side? What?
It's a 100 to 1 shot that I get the dollar. I wonder
what she went out for. I guess she's gone to tell
Mrs. Muldoon on the second floor, that we're recon-

ciled. I'll remember this. Soft soap! And Ragsy was talking about slugging her!"

Mrs. Peters came back with a bottle of sarsaparilla.

"I'm glad I happened to have that dollar," she said. "You're all run down, honey."

Mr. Peters had a tablespoonful of the stuff inserted into him. Then Mrs. Peters sat on his lap and murmured:

"Call me tootsum wootsums again, James."

He sat still, held there by his materialized goddess of spring.

Spring had come.

On the bench in Union Square Mr. Ragsdale and Mr. Kidd squirmed, tongue-parched, awaiting D'Artagnan and his dollar.

"I wish I had choked her at first," said Mr. Peters to himself.

WHILE THE AUTO WAITS

PROMPTLY at the beginning of twilight, came
again to that quiet corner of that quiet, small park
the girl in gray. She sat upon a bench and read a
book, for there was yet to come a half hour in which
print could be accomplished.

To repeat: Her dress was gray, and plain enough
to mask its impeccancy of style and fit. A large-
meshed veil imprisoned her turban hat and a face
that shone through it with a calm and unconscious
beauty. She had come there at the same hour on the
day previous, and on the day before that; and there
was one who knew it.

The young man who knew it hovered near, relying
upon burnt sacrifices to the great joss, Luck. His
piety was rewarded, for, in turning a page, her book
slipped from her fingers and bounded from the bench
a full yard away.

The young man pounced upon it with instant avid-
ity, returning it to its owner with that air that seems
to flourish in parks and public places — a compound
of gallantry and hope, tempered with respect for the
policeman on the beat. In a pleasant voice, he risked
an inconsequent remark upon the weather — that in-

troductory topic responsible for so much of the world's unhappiness — and stood poised for a moment, awaiting his fate.

The girl looked him over leisurely; at his ordinary, neat dress and his features distinguished by nothing particular in the way of expression.

"You may sit down, if you like," she said, in a full, deliberate contralto. "Really, I would like to have you do so. The light is too bad for reading. I would prefer to talk."

The vassal of Luck slid upon the seat by her side with complaisance.

"Do you know," he said, speaking the formula with which park chairmen open their meetings, "that you are quite the stunningest girl I have seen in a long time? I had my eye on you yesterday. Didn't know somebody was bowled over by those pretty lamps of yours, did you, honeysuckle?"

"Whoever you are," said the girl, in icy tones, "you must remember that I am a lady. I will excuse the remark you have just made because the mistake was, doubtless, not an unnatural one — in your circle. I asked you to sit down; if the invitation must constitute me your honeysuckle, consider it withdrawn."

"I earnestly beg your pardon," pleaded the young man. His expression of satisfaction had changed to one of penitence and humility. "It was my fault, you know — I mean, there are girls in parks, you know — that is, of course, you don't know, but —— "

" Abandon the subject, if you please. Of course I know. Now, tell me about these people passing and crowding, each way, along these paths. Where are they going? Why do they hurry so? Are they happy? "

The young man had promptly abandoned his air of coquetry. His cue was now for a waiting part; he could not guess the rôle he would be expected to play.

" It *is* interesting to watch them," he replied, postulating her mood. " It is the wonderful drama of life. Some are going to supper and some to — er — other places. One wonders what their histories are."

" I do not," said the girl; " I am not so inquisitive. I come here to sit because here, only, can I be near the great, common, throbbing heart of humanity. My part in life is cast where its beats are never felt. Can you surmise why I spoke to you, Mr.——? "

" Parkenstacker," supplied the young man. Then he looked eager and hopeful.

" No," said the girl, holding up a slender finger, and smiling slightly. " You would recognize it immediately. It is impossible to keep one's name out of print. Or even one's portrait. This veil and this hat of my maid furnish me with an *incog*. You should have seen the chauffeur stare at it when he thought I did not see. Candidly, there are five or six names that belong in the holy of holies, and mine, by the accident of birth, is one of them. I spoke to you, Mr. Stackenpot —— "

" Parkenstacker," corrected the young man, modestly.

"— Mr. Parkenstacker, because I wanted to talk, for once, with a natural man — one unspoiled by the despicable gloss of wealth and supposed social superiority. Oh! you do not know how weary I am of it — money, money, money! And of the men who surround me, dancing like little marionettes all cut by the same pattern. I am sick of pleasure, of jewels, of travel, of society, of luxuries of all kinds."

" I always had an idea," ventured the young man, hesitatingly, " that money must be a pretty good thing."

" A competence is to be desired. But when you have so many millions that ——! " She concluded the sentence with a gesture of despair. " It is the monotony of it," she continued, " that palls. Drives, dinners, theatres, balls, suppers, with the gilding of superfluous wealth over it all. Sometimes the very tinkle of the ice in my champagne glass nearly drives me mad."

Mr. Parkenstacker looked ingenuously interested.

" I have always liked," he said, " to read and hear

about the ways of wealthy and fashionable folks. I
suppose I am a bit of a snob. But I like to have my
information accurate. Now, I had formed the opinion that champagne is cooled in the bottle and not by
placing ice in the glass."

The girl gave a musical laugh of genuine amusement.

"You should know," she explained, in an indul-
gent tone, "that we of the non-useful class depend
for our amusement upon departure from precedent.
Just now it is a fad to put ice in champagne. The
idea was originated by a visiting Prince of Tartary
while dining at the Waldorf. It will soon give way
to some other whim. Just as at a dinner party this
week on Madison Avenue a green kid glove was laid
by the plate of each guest to be put on and used while
eating olives."

"I see," admitted the young man, humbly.
"These special diversions of the inner circle do not
become familiar to the common public."

"Sometimes," continued the girl, acknowledging
his confession of error by a slight bow, "I have
thought that if I ever should love a man it would be
one of lowly station. One who is a worker and not a
drone. But, doubtless, the claims of caste and wealth
will prove stronger than my inclination. Just now
I am besieged by two. One is a Grand Duke of a
German principality. I think he has, or has had, a

wife, somewhere, driven mad by his intemperance and cruelty. The other is an English Marquis, so cold and mercenary that I even prefer the diabolism of the Duke. What is it that impels me to tell you these things, Mr. Packenstacker? "

" Parkenstacker," breathed the young man. " Indeed, you cannot know how much I appreciate your confidences."

The girl contemplated him with the calm, impersonal regard that befitted the difference in their stations.

" What is your line of business, Mr. Parkenstacker? " she asked.

" A very humble one. But I hope to rise in the world. Were you really in earnest when you said that you could love a man of lowly position? "

" Indeed I was. But I said ' might.' There is the Grand Duke and the Marquis, you know. Yes; no calling could be too humble were the man what I would wish him to be."

" I work," declared Mr. Parkenstacker, " in a restaurant."

The girl shrank slightly.

" Not as a waiter? " she said, a little imploringly. " Labor is noble, but — personal attendance, you know — valets and —— "

" I am not a waiter. I am cashier in " — on the street they faced that bounded the opposite side of

the park was the brilliant electric sign " RESTAU-
RANT " — " I am cashier in that restaurant you see
there."

The girl consulted a tiny watch set in a bracelet of
rich design upon her left wrist, and rose, hurriedly.
She thrust her book into a glittering reticule suspended from her waist, for which, however, the book
was too large.

" Why are you not at work? " she asked.

" I am on the night turn," said the young man;
" it is yet an hour before my period begins. May I
not hope to see you again? "

" I do not know. Perhaps — but the whim may
not seize me again. I must go quickly now. There
is a dinner, and a box at the play — and, oh! the
same old round. Perhaps you noticed an automobile
at the upper corner of the park as you came. One
with a white body."

" And red running gear? " asked the young man,
knitting his brows reflectively.

" Yes. I always come in that. Pierre waits for
me there. He supposes me to be shopping in the department store across the square. Conceive of the
bondage of the life wherein we must deceive even our
chauffeurs. Good-night."

" But it is dark now," said Mr. Parkenstacker,
" and the park is full of rude men. May I not
walk —— ? "

" If you have the slightest regard for my wishes,"
said the girl, firmly, " you will remain at this bench
for ten minutes after I have left. I do not mean to
accuse you, but you are probably aware that autos
generally bear the monogram of their owner. Again,
good-night."

Swift and stately she moved away through the
dusk. The young man watched her graceful form
as she reached the pavement at the park's edge, and
turned up along it toward the corner where stood the
automobile. Then he treacherously and unhesitatingly began to dodge and skim among the park trees
and shrubbery in a course parallel to her route, keeping her well in sight.

When she reached the corner she turned her head
to glance at the motor car, and then passed it, con-
tinuing on across the street. Sheltered behind a convenient standing cab, the young man followed her
movements closely with his eyes. Passing down the
sidewalk of the street opposite the park, she entered
the restaurant with the blazing sign. The place was
one of those frankly glaring establishments, all white
paint and glass, where one may dine cheaply and
conspicuously. The girl penetrated the restaurant to
some retreat at its rear, whence she quickly emerged
without her hat and veil.

The cashier's desk was well to the front. A red-
haired girl on the stool climbed down, glancing

pointedly at the clock as she did so. The girl in gray mounted in her place.

The young man thrust his hands into his pockets and walked slowly back along the sidewalk. At the corner his foot struck a small, paper-covered volume lying there, sending it sliding to the edge of the turf. By its picturesque cover he recognized it as the book the girl had been reading. He picked it up carelessly, and saw that its title was " New Arabian Nights," the author being of the name of Stevenson. He dropped it again upon the grass, and lounged, irresolute, for a minute. Then he stepped into the automobile, reclined upon the cushions, and said two words to the chauffeur:

" Club, Henri."

A COMEDY IN RUBBER

ONE may hope, in spite of the metaphorists, to avoid the breath of the deadly upas tree; one may, by great good fortune, succeed in blacking the eye of the basilisk; one might even dodge the attentions of Cerberus and Argus, but no man, alive or dead, can escape the gaze of the Rubberer.

New York is the Caoutchouc City. There are many, of course, who go their ways, making money, without turning to the right or the left, but there is a tribe abroad wonderfully composed, like the Martians, solely of eyes and means of locomotion.

These devotees of curiosity swarm, like flies, in a moment in a struggling, breathless circle about the scene of an unusual occurrence. If a workman opens a manhole, if a street car runs over a man from North Tarrytown, if a little boy drops an egg on his way home from the grocery, if a casual house or two drops into the subway, if a lady loses a nickel through a hole in the lisle thread, if the police drag a telephone and a racing chart forth from an Ibsen Society reading-room, if Senator Depew or Mr. Chuck Connors walks out to take the air — if any of these incidents or accidents takes place, you will see the mad, irresistible rush of the "rubber" tribe to the spot.

The importance of the event does not count. They gaze with equal interest and absorption at a chorus girl or at a man painting a liver pill sign. They will form as deep a cordon around a man with a clubfoot as they will around a balked automobile. They have the furor rubberendi. They are optical gluttons, feasting and fattening on the misfortunes of their fellow beings. They gloat and pore and glare and squint and stare with their fishy eyes like goggle-eyed perch at the hook baited with calamity.

It would seem that Cupid would find these ocular vampires too cold game for his calorific shafts, but have we not yet to discover an immune even among the Protozoa? Yes, beautiful Romance descended upon two of this tribe, and love came into their hearts as they crowded about the prostrate form of a man who had been run over by a brewery wagon.

William Pry was the first on the spot. He was an expert at such gatherings. With an expression of intense happiness on his features, he stood over the victim of the accident, listening to his groans as if to the sweetest music. When the crowd of spectators had swelled to a closely packed circle William saw a violent commotion in the crowd opposite him. Men were hurled aside like ninepins by the impact of some moving body that clove them like the rush of a tornado. With elbows, umbrella, hat-pin, tongue, and fingernails doing their duty, Violet Seymour forced her way through the mob of onlookers to the first row. Strong men who even had been able to secure a seat on the 5.30 Harlem express staggered back like children as she bucked centre. Two large lady spectators who had seen the Duke of Roxburgh married and had often blocked traffic on Twenty-third Street fell back into the second row with ripped shirt-waists when Violet had finished with them. William Pry loved her at first sight.

The ambulance removed the unconscious agent of Cupid. William and Violet remained after the crowd had dispersed. They were true Rubberers. People who leave the scene of an accident with the ambulance have not genuine caoutchouc in the cosmogony of their necks. The delicate, fine flavor of the affair is to be had only in the after-taste — in gloating over the spot, in gazing fixedly at the houses opposite, in hovering there in a dream more exquisite than the opium-eater's ecstasy. William Pry and Violet Seymour were connoisseurs in casualties. They knew how to extract full enjoyment from every incident.

Presently they looked at each other. Violet had a brown birthmark on her neck as large as a silver half-dollar. William fixed his eyes upon it. William Pry had inordinately bowed legs. Violet allowed her

gaze to linger unswervingly upon them.   Face to face
they stood thus for moments, each staring at the
other.   Etiquette would not allow them to speak; but
in the Caoutchouc City it is permitted to gaze without stint at the trees in the parks and at the physi-
cal blemishes of a fellow creature.

At length with a sigh they parted.   But Cupid had
been the driver of the brewery wagon, and the wheel
that broke a leg united two fond hearts.

The next meeting of the hero and heroine was in
front of a board fence near Broadway.   The day had
been a disappointing one.   There had been no fights
on the street, children had kept from under the wheels
of the street cars, cripples and fat men in negligée
shirts were scarce; nobody seemed to be inclined to
slip on banana peels or fall down with heart disease.
Even the sport from Kokomo, Ind., who claims to
be a cousin of ex-Mayor Low and scatters nickels
from a cab window, had not put in his appearance.
There was nothing to stare at, and William Pry had
premonitions of ennui.

But he saw a large crowd scrambling and pushing
excitedly in front of a billboard.   Sprinting for it,
he knocked down an old woman and a child carrying
a bottle of milk, and fought his way like a demon into
the mass of spectators.   Already in the inner line
stood Violet Seymour with one sleeve and two gold fill-
ings gone, a corset steel puncture and a sprained

wrist, but happy. She was looking at what there
was to see. A man was painting upon the fence:
" Eat Bricklets — They Fill Your Face."

Violet blushed when she saw William Pry. William
jabbed a lady in a black silk raglan in the ribs, kicked
a boy in the shin, hit an old gentleman on the left ear
and managed to crowd nearer to Violet. They stood
for an hour looking at the man paint the letters.
Then William's love could be repressed no longer.
He touched her on the arm.

" Come with me," he said. " I know where there
is a bootblack without an Adam's apple."

She looked up at him shyly, yet with unmistakable
love transfiguring her countenance.

" And you have saved it for me? " she asked,
trembling with the first dim ecstasy of a woman be-
loved.

Together they hurried to the bootblack's stand.
An hour they spent there gazing at the malformed
youth.

A window-cleaner fell from the fifth story to the
sidewalk beside them. As the ambulance came clang-
ing up William pressed her hand joyously. " Four
ribs at least and a compound fracture," he whispered,
swiftly. " You are not sorry that you met me, are
you, dearest? "

" Me?" said Violet, returning the pressure. " Sure
not. I could stand all day rubbering with you."

The climax of the romance occurred a few days later. Perhaps the reader will remember the intense excitement into which the city was thrown when Eliza Jane, a colored woman, was served with a subpœna. The Rubber Tribe encamped on the spot. With his own hands William Pry placed a board upon two beer kegs in the street opposite Eliza Jane's residence. He and Violet sat there for three days and nights. Then it occurred to a detective to open the door and serve the subpœna. He sent for a kinetoscope and did so.

Two souls with such congenial tastes could not long remain apart. As a policeman drove them away with his night stick that evening they plighted their troth. The seeds of love had been well sown, and had grown up, hardy and vigorous, into a — let us call it a rubber plant.

The wedding of William Pry and Violet Seymour was set for June 10. The Big Church in the Middle of the Block was banked high with flowers. The populous tribe of Rubberers the world over is rampant over weddings. They are the pessimists of the pews. They are the guyers of the groom and the banterers of the bride. They come to laugh at your marriage, and should you escape from Hymen's tower on the back of death's pale steed they will come to the funeral and sit in the same pew and cry over your luck. Rubber will stretch.

The church was lighted. A grosgrain carpet lay over the asphalt to the edge of the sidewalk. Bridesmaids were patting one another's sashes awry and speaking of the Bride's freckles. Coachmen tied white ribbons on their whips and bewailed the space of time between drinks. The minister was musing over his possible fee, essaying conjecture whether it would suffice to purchase a new broadcloth suit for himself and a photograph of Laura Jane Libbey for his wife. Yea, Cupid was in the air.

And outside the church, oh, my brothers, surged and heaved the rank and file of the tribe of Rubberers. In two bodies they were, with the grosgrain carpet and cops with clubs between. They crowded like cattle, they fought, they pressed and surged and swayed and trampled one another to see a bit of a girl in a white veil acquire license to go through a man's pockets while he sleeps.

But the hour for the wedding came and went, and the bride and bridegroom came not. And impatience gave way to alarm and alarm brought about search, and they were not found. And then two big policemen took a hand and dragged out of the furious mob of onlookers a crushed and trampled thing, with a wedding ring in its vest pocket and a shredded and hysterical woman beating her way to the carpet's edge, ragged, bruised and obstreperous.

William Pry and Violet Seymour, creatures of

habit, had joined in the seething game of the spectators, unable to resist the overwhelming desire to gaze
upon themselves entering, as bride and bridegroom,
the rose-decked church.

Rubber will out.

ONE THOUSAND DOLLARS

ONE thousand dollars," repeated Lawyer Tolman, solemnly and severely, " and here is the money."

Young Gillian gave a decidedly amused laugh as he fingered the thin package of new fifty-dollar notes.

" It's such a confoundedly awkward amount," he explained, genially, to the lawyer. " If it had been ten thousand a fellow might wind up with a lot of fireworks and do himself credit. Even fifty dollars would have been less trouble."

" You heard the reading of your uncle's will," continued Lawyer Tolman, professionally dry in his tones. " I do not know if you paid much attention to its details. I must remind you of one. You are required to render to us an account of the manner of expenditure of this $1,000 as soon as you have disposed of it. The will stipulates that. I trust that you will so far comply with the late Mr. Gillian's wishes."

" You may depend upon it," said the young man, politely, " in spite of the extra expense it will entail. I may have to engage a secretary. I was never good at accounts."

Gillian went to his club. There he hunted out one whom he called Old Bryson.

Old Bryson was calm and forty and sequestered. He was in a corner reading a book, and when he saw Gillian approaching he sighed, laid down his book and took off his glasses.

"Old Bryson, wake up," said Gillian. "I've a funny story to tell you."

"I wish you would tell it to some one in the billiard room," said Old Bryson. "You know how I hate your stories."

"This is a better one than usual," said Gillian, rolling a cigarette; "and I'm glad to tell it to you. It's too sad and funny to go with the rattling of billiard balls. I've just come from my late uncle's firm of legal corsairs. He leaves me an even thousand dollars. Now, what can a man possibly do with a thousand dollars?"

"I thought," said Old Bryson, showing as much interest as a bee shows in a vinegar cruet, "that the late Septimus Gillian was worth something like half a million."

"He was," assented Gillian, joyously, "and that's where the joke comes in. He's left his whole cargo of doubloons to a microbe. That is, part of it goes to the man who invents a new bacillus and the rest to establish a hospital for doing away with it again. There are one or two trifling bequests on the side. The butler and the housekeeper get a seal ring and $10 each. His nephew gets $1,000."

"You've always had plenty of money to spend," observed Old Bryson.

"Tons," said Gillian. "Uncle was the fairygodmother as far as an allowance was concerned."

"Any other heirs?" asked Old Bryson.

"None." Gillian frowned at his cigarette and kicked the upholstered leather of a divan uneasily. "There is a Miss Hayden, a ward of my uncle, who lived in his house. She's a quiet thing — musical — the daughter of somebody who was unlucky enough to be his friend. I forgot to say that she was in on the seal ring and $10 joke, too. I wish I had been. Then I could have had two bottles of brut, tipped the waiter with the ring and had the whole business off my hands. Don't be superior and insulting, Old Bryson — tell me what a fellow can do with a thousand dollars."

Old Bryson rubbed his glasses and smiled. And when Old Bryson smiled, Gillian knew that he intended to be more offensive than ever.

"A thousand dollars," he said, "means much or little. One man may buy a happy home with it and laugh at Rockefeller. Another could send his wife South with it and save her life. A thousand dollars would buy pure milk for one hundred babies during June, July, and August and save fifty of their lives. You could count upon a half hour's diversion with it at faro in one of the fortified art galleries. It would furnish an education to an ambitious boy. I am told that a genuine Corot was secured for that amount in an auction room yesterday. You could move to a New Hampshire town and live respectably two years on it. You could rent Madison Square Garden for one evening with it, and lecture your audience, if you should have one, on the precariousness of the profession of heir presumptive."

"People might like you, Old Bryson," said Gillian, always unruffled, "if you wouldn't moralize. I asked you to tell me what I could do with a thousand dollars."

"You?" said Bryson, with a gentle laugh. "Why, Bobby Gillian, there's only one logical thing you could do. You can go buy Miss Lotta Lauriere a diamond pendant with the money, and then take yourself off to Idaho and inflict your presence upon a ranch. I advise a sheep ranch, as I have a particular dislike for sheep."

"Thanks," said Gillian, rising, "I thought I could depend upon you, Old Bryson. You've hit on the very scheme. I wanted to chuck the money in a lump, for I've got to turn in an account for it, and I hate itemizing."

Gillian phoned for a cab and said to the driver:

"The stage entrance of the Columbine Theatre."

Miss Lotta Lauriere was assisting nature with a powder puff, almost ready for her call at a crowded matinée, when her dresser mentioned the name of Mr. Gillian.

" Let it in," said Miss Lauriere. " Now, what is it, Bobby? I'm going on in two minutes."

" Rabbit-foot your right ear a little," suggested Gillian, critically. " That's better. It won't take two minutes for me. What do you say to a little thing in the pendant line? I can stand three ciphers with a figure one in front of 'em."

" Oh, just as you say," carolled Miss Lauriere. " My right glove, Adams. Say, Bobby, did you see that necklace Della Stacey had on the other night? Twenty-two hundred dollars it cost at Tiffany's. But, of course — pull my sash a little to the left, Adams."

" Miss Lauriere for the opening chorus! " cried the call boy without.

Gillian strolled out to where his cab was waiting.

" What would you do with a thousand dollars if you had it? " he asked the driver.

" Open a s'loon," said the cabby, promptly and huskily. " I know a place I could take money in with both hands. It's a four-story brick on a corner. I've got it figured out. Second story — Chinks and chop suey; third floor — manicures and foreign missions; fourth floor — poolroom. If you was thinking of putting up the cap —— "

" Oh, no," said Gillian, " I merely asked from curiosity. I take you by the hour. Drive till I tell you to stop."

Eight blocks down Broadway Gillian poked up the trap with his cane and got out. A blind man sat upon a stool on the sidewalk selling pencils. Gillian went out and stood before him.

" Excuse me," he said, " but would you mind telling me what you would do if you had a thousand dollars? "

" You got out of that cab that just drove up, didn't you? " asked the blind man.

" I did," said Gillian.

" I guess you are all right," said the pencil dealer, " to ride in a cab by daylight. Take a look at that, if you like."

He drew a small book from his coat pocket and held it out. Gillian opened it and saw that it was a bank deposit book. It showed a balance of $1,785 to the blind man's credit.

Gillian returned the book and got into the cab.

" I forgot something," he said. " You may drive to the law offices of Tolman & Sharp, at —— Broadway."

Lawyer Tolman looked at him hostilely and inquiringly through his gold-rimmed glasses.

" I beg your pardon," said Gillian, cheerfully, " but may I ask you a question? It is not an impertinent one, I hope. Was Miss Hayden left anything by my uncle's will besides the ring and the $10?"

"Nothing," said Mr. Tolman.

"I thank you very much, sir," said Gillian, and out he went to his cab. He gave the driver the address of his late uncle's home.

Miss Hayden was writing letters in the library. She was small and slender and clothed in black. But you would have noticed her eyes. Gillian drifted in with his air of regarding the world as inconsequent.

"I've just come from old Tolman's," he explained. "They've been going over the papers down there. They found a " — Gillian searched his memory for a legal term — "they found an amendment or a postscript or something to the will. It seemed that the old boy loosened up a little on second thoughts and willed you a thousand dollars. I was driving up this way and Tolman asked me to bring you the money. Here it is. You'd better count it to see if it's right." Gillian laid the money beside her hand on the desk.

Miss Hayden turned white. "Oh!" she said, and again "Oh!"

Gillian half turned and looked out the window.

"I suppose, of course," he said, in a low voice, "that you know I love you."

"I am sorry," said Miss Hayden, taking up her money.

"There is no use?" asked Gillian, almost light-heartedly.

"I am sorry," she said again.

"May I write a note?" asked Gillian, with a smile. He seated himself at the big library table. She supplied him with paper and pen, and then went back to her secrétaire.

Gillian made out his account of his expenditure of the thousand dollars in these words:

"Paid by the black sheep, Robert Gillian, $1,000 on account of the eternal happiness, owed by Heaven to the best and dearest woman on earth."

Gillian slipped his writing into an envelope, bowed and went his way.

His cab stopped again at the offices of Tolman & Sharp.

"I have expended the thousand dollars," he said, cheerily, to Tolman of the gold glasses, "and I have come to render account of it, as I agreed. There is quite a feeling of summer in the air — do you not think so, Mr. Tolman?" He tossed a white envelope on the lawyer's table. "You will find there a memorandum, sir, of the *modus operandi* of the vanishing of the dollars."

Without touching the envelope, Mr. Tolman went to a door and called his partner, Sharp. Together they explored the caverns of an immense safe. Forth they dragged as trophy of their search a big envelope sealed with wax. This they forcibly invaded, and wagged their venerable heads together over its contents. Then Tolman became spokesman.

" Mr. Gillian," he said, formally, " there was a codicil to your uncle's will. It was intrusted to us privately, with instructions that it be not opened until you had furnished us with a full account of your handling of the $1,000 bequest in the will. As you have fulfilled the conditions, my partner and I have read the codicil. I do not wish to encumber your understanding with its legal phraseology, but I will acquaint you with the spirit of its contents.

" In the event that your disposition of the $1,000 demonstrates that you possess any of the qualifications that deserve reward, much benefit will accrue to you. Mr. Sharp and I are named as the judges, and I assure you that we will do our duty strictly according to justice — with liberality. We are not at all unfavorably disposed toward you, Mr. Gillian. But let us return to the letter of the codicil. If your disposal of the money in question has been prudent, wise, or unselfish, it is in our power to hand you over bonds to the value of $50,000, which have been placed in our hands for that purpose. But if — as our client, the late Mr. Gillian, explicitly provides — you have used this money as you have used money in the past — I quote the late Mr. Gillian — in reprehensible dissipation among disreputable associates — the $50,000 is to be paid to Miriam Hayden, ward of the late Mr. Gillian, without delay. Now, Mr. Gillian, Mr. Sharp and I will examine your account in regard to the $1,000. You submit it in writing, I believe. I hope you will repose confidence in our decision."

Mr. Tolman reached for the envelope. Gillian was a little the quicker in taking it up. He tore the account and its cover leisurely into strips and dropped them into his pocket.

" It's all right," he said, smilingly. " There isn't a bit of need to bother you with this. I don't suppose you'd understand these itemized bets, anyway. I lost the thousand dollars on the races. Good-day to you, gentlemen."

Tolman & Sharp shook their heads mournfully at each other when Gillian left, for they heard him whistling gayly in the hallway as he waited for the elevator.

THE DEFEAT OF THE CITY

ROBERT WALMSLEY'S descent upon the city resulted in a Kilkenny struggle. He came out of the fight victor by a fortune and a reputation. On the other hand, he was swallowed up by the city. The city gave him what he demanded and then branded him with its brand. It remodelled, cut, trimmed and stamped him to the pattern it approves. It opened its social gates to him and shut him in on a close-cropped, formal lawn with the select herd of ruminants. In dress, habits, manners, provincialism, routine and narrowness he acquired that charming insolence, that irritating completeness, that sophisticated crassness, that overbalanced poise that makes the Manhattan gentleman so delightfully small in his greatness.

One of the up-state rural counties pointed with pride to the successful young metropolitan lawyer as a product of its soil. Six years earlier this county had removed the wheat straw from between its huckle-berry-stained teeth and emitted a derisive and bucolic laugh as old man Walmsley's freckle-faced " Bob " abandoned the certain three-per-diem meals of the one-horse farm for the discontinuous quick lunch counters of the three-ringed metropolis. At the end of the six years no murder trial, coaching party, automobile accident or cotillion was complete in which the name of Robert Walmsley did not figure.   Tailors waylaid him in the street to get a new wrinkle from the cut of his unwrinkled trousers.   Hyphenated fellows in the clubs and members of the oldest subpœnaed families were glad to clap him on the back and allow him three letters of his name.

But the Matterhorn of Robert Walmsley's success was not scaled until he married Alicia Van Der Pool. I cite the Matterhorn, for just so high and cool and white and inaccessible was this daughter of the old burghers.   The social Alps that ranged about her — over whose bleak passes a thousand climbers struggled — reached only to her knees.   She towered in her own atmosphere, serene, chaste, prideful, wading in no fountains, dining no monkeys, breeding no dogs for bench shows.   She was a Van Der Pool.   Fountains were made to play for her; monkeys were made for other people's ancestors; dogs, she understood, were created to be companions of blind persons and objectionable characters who smoked pipes.

This was the Matterhorn that Robert Walmsley accomplished.   If he found, with the good poet with the game foot and artificially curled hair, that he who ascends to mountain tops will find the loftiest peaks most wrapped in clouds and snow, he concealed his chilblains beneath a brave and smiling exterior.   He was a lucky man and knew it, even though he were imitating the Spartan boy with an ice-cream freezer beneath his doublet frappéeing the region of his heart.

After a brief wedding tour abroad, the couple returned to create a decided ripple in the calm cistern (so placid and cool and sunless it is) of the best society. They entertained at their red brick mausoleum of ancient greatness in an old square that is a cemetery of crumbled glory. And Robert Walmsley was proud of his wife; although while one of his hands shook his guests' the other held tightly to his alpenstock and thermometer.

One day Alicia found a letter written to Robert by his mother. It was an unerudite letter, full of crops and motherly love and farm notes. It chronicled the health of the pig and the recent red calf, and asked concerning Robert's in return. It was a letter direct from the soil, straight from home, full of biographies of bees, tales of turnips, pæans of new-laid eggs, neglected parents and the slump in dried apples.

"Why have I not been shown your mother's letters?" asked Alicia. There was always something in her voice that made you think of lorgnettes, of accounts at Tiffany's, of sledges smoothly gliding on the trail from Dawson to Forty Mile, of the tinkling of pendant prisms on your grandmothers' chandeliers, of snow lying on a convent roof; of a police sergeant

refusing bail. " Your mother," continued Alicia,
" invites us to make a visit to the farm. I have
never seen a farm. We will go there for a week or
two, Robert."

" We will," said Robert, with the grand air of an
associate Supreme Justice concurring in an opinion.
" I did not lay the invitation before you because I
thought you would not care to go. I am much pleased
at your decision."

" I will write to her myself," answered Alicia, with
a faint foreshadowing of enthusiasm. " Félice shall
pack my trunks at once. Seven, I think, will be
enough. I do not suppose that your mother entertains
a great deal. Does she give many house parties? "

Robert arose, and as attorney for rural places filed
a demurrer against six of the seven trunks. He en-
deavored to define, picture, elucidate, set forth and
describe a farm. His own words sounded strange in
his ears. He had not realized how thoroughly urbsi-
dized he had become.

· A week passed and found them landed at the little
country station five hours out from the city. A grin-
ning, stentorian, sarcastic youth driving a mule to a
spring wagon hailed Robert savagely.

" Hallo, Mr. Walmsley. Found your way back at
last, have you? Sorry I couldn't bring in the automobile for you, but dad's bull-tonguing the ten-acre
clover patch with it to-day. Guess you'll excuse my

not wearing a dress suit over to meet you — it ain't six o'clock yet, you know."

"I'm glad to see you, Tom," said Robert, grasping his brother's hand. "Yes, I've found my way at last. You've a right to say 'at last.' It's been over two years since the last time. But it will be oftener after this, my boy."

Alicia, cool in the summer heat as an Arctic wraith, white as a Norse snow maiden in her flimsy muslin and fluttering lace parasol, came round the corner of the station; and Tom was stripped of his assurance. He became chiefly eyesight clothed in blue jeans, and on the homeward drive to the mule alone did he confide in language the inwardness of his thoughts.

They drove homeward. The low sun dropped a spendthrift flood of gold upon the fortunate fields of wheat. The cities were far away. The road lay curling around wood and dale and hill like a ribbon lost from the robe of careless summer. The wind followed like a whinnying colt in the track of Phœbus's steeds.

By and by the farmhouse peeped gray out of its faithful grove; they saw the long lane with its convoy of walnut trees running from the road to the house; they smelled the wild rose and the breath of cool, damp willows in the creek's bed. And then in unison all the voices of the soil began a chant addressed to the soul of Robert Walmsley. Out of the tilted aisles of the dim wood they came hollowly; they chirped and

buzzed from the parched grass; they trilled from the
ripples of the creek ford; they floated up in clear
Pan's pipe notes from the dimming meadows; the
whippoorwills joined in as they pursued midges in the
upper air; slow-going cow-bells struck out a homely
accompaniment — and this was what each one said:
" You've found your way back at last, have you? "

The old voices of the soil spoke to him.   Leaf and
bud and blossom conversed with him in the old vocabulary of his careless youth — the inanimate things, the
familiar stones and rails, the gates and furrows and
roofs and turns of the road had an eloquence, too, and
a power in the transformation.   The country had
smiled and he had felt the breath of it, and his heart
was drawn as if in a moment back to his old love.
The city was far away.

This rural atavism, then, seized Robert Walmsley
and possessed him.   A queer thing he noticed in connection with it was that Alicia, sitting at his side,
suddenly seemed to him a stranger.   She did not belong to this recurrent phase.   Never before had she
seemed so remote, so colorless and high — so intan-
gible and unreal.   And yet he had never admired her
more than when she sat there by him in the rickety
spring wagon, chiming no more with his mood and
with her environment than the Matterhorn chimes
with a peasant's cabbage garden.

That night when the greetings and the supper were

over, the entire family, including Buff, the yellow dog, bestrewed itself upon the front porch. Alicia, not haughty but silent, sat in the shadow dressed in an exquisite pale-gray tea gown. Robert's mother discoursed to her happily concerning marmalade and lumbago. Tom sat on the top step; Sisters Millie and Pam on the lowest step to catch the lightning bugs. Mother had the willow rocker. Father sat in the big armchair with one of its arms gone. Buff sprawled in the middle of the porch in everybody's way. The twilight pixies and pucks stole forth unseen and plunged other poignant shafts of memory into the heart of Robert. A rural madness entered his soul. The city was far away.

Father sat without his pipe, writhing in his heavy boots, a sacrifice to rigid courtesy. Robert shouted: " No, you don't! " He fetched the pipe and lit it; he seized the old gentleman's boots and tore them off. The last one slipped suddenly, and Mr. Robert Walmsley, of Washington Square, tumbled off the porch backward with Buff on top of him, howling fearfully. Tom laughed sarcastically.

Robert tore off his coat and vest and hurled them into a lilac bush.

" Come out here, you landlubber," he cried to Tom, " and I'll put grass seed on your back. I think you called me a ' dude ' a while ago. Come along and cut your capers."

Tom understood the invitation and accepted it with
delight. Three times they wrestled on the grass,
" side holds," even as the giants of the mat. And
twice was Tom forced to bite grass at the hands of
the distinguished lawyer. Dishevelled, panting, each
still boasting of his own prowess, they stumbled back
to the porch. Millie cast a pert reflection upon the
qualities of a city brother. In an instant Robert had
secured a horrid katydid in his fingers and bore down
upon her. Screaming wildly, she fled up the lane,
pursued by the avenging glass of form. A quarter
of a mile and they returned, she full of apology to
the victorious " dude." The rustic mania possessed
him unabatedly.

" I can do up a cowpenful of you slow hayseeds,"
he proclaimed, vaingloriously. " Bring on your bull-
dogs, your hired men and your log-rollers."

He turned handsprings on the grass that prodded
Tom to envious sarcasm. And then, with a whoop,
he clattered to the rear and brought back Uncle Ike,
a battered colored retainer of the family, with his
banjo, and strewed sand on the porch and danced
" Chicken in the Bread Tray " and did buck-and-
wing wonders for half an hour longer. Incredibly
wild and boisterous things he did. He sang, he told
stories that set all but one shrieking, he played the
yokel, the humorous clodhopper ; he was mad, mad
with the revival of the old life in his blood.

He became so extravagant that once his mother sought gently to reprove him. Then Alicia moved as though she were about to speak, but she did not. Through it all she sat immovable, a slim, white spirit in the dusk that no man might question or read.

By and by she asked permission to ascend to her room, saying that she was tired. On her way she passed Robert. He was standing in the door, the figure of vulgar comedy, with ruffled hair, reddened face and unpardonable confusion of attire — no trace there of the immaculate Robert Walmsley, the courted clubman and ornament of select circles. He was doing a conjuring trick with some household utensils, and the family, now won over to him without exception, was beholding him with worshipful admiration.

As Alicia passed in Robert started suddenly. He had forgotten for the moment that she was present. Without a glance at him she went on upstairs.

After that the fun grew quiet. An hour passed in talk, and then Robert went up himself.

She was standing by the window when he entered their room. She was still clothed as when they were on the porch. Outside and crowding against the window was a giant apple tree, full blossomed.

Robert sighed and went near the window. He was ready to meet his fate. A confessed vulgarian, he foresaw the verdict of justice in the shape of that still, whiteclad form. He knew the rigid lines that a

Van Der Pool would draw. He was a peasant gam-
bolling indecorously in the valley, and the pure, cold,
white, unthawed summit of the Matterhorn could not
but frown on him. He had been unmasked by his
own actions. All the polish, the poise, the form that
the city had given him had fallen from him like an
ill-fitting mantle at the first breath of a country
breeze. Dully he awaited the approaching condemna-
tion.

"Robert," said the calm, cool voice of his judge,
"I thought I married a gentleman."

Yes, it was coming. And yet, in the face of it,
Robert Walmsley was eagerly regarding a certain
branch of the apple tree upon which he used to climb
out of that very window. He believed he could do it
now. He wondered how many blossoms there were
on the tree — ten millions? But here was some one
speaking again:

"I thought I married a gentleman," the voice
went on, "but——"

Why had she come and was standing so close by
his side?

"But I find that I have married"—was this
Alicia talking?—"something better — a man —
Bob, dear, kiss me, won't you?"

The city was far away.

THE SHOCKS OF DOOM

THERE is an aristocracy of the public parks and even of the vagabonds who use them for their private apartments. Vallance felt rather than knew this, but when he stepped down out of his world into chaos his feet brought him directly to Madison Square.

Raw and astringent as a schoolgirl — of the old order — young May breathed austerely among the budding trees. Vallance buttoned his coat, lighted his last cigarette and took his seat upon a bench. For three minutes he mildly regretted the last hundred of his last thousand that it had cost him when the bicycle cop put an end to his last automobile ride. Then he felt in every pocket and found not a single penny. He had given up his apartment that morning. His furniture had gone toward certain debts. His clothes, save what were upon him, had descended to his man-servant for back wages. As he sat there was not in the whole city for him a bed or a broiled lobster or a street-car fare or a carnation for his buttonhole unless he should obtain them by sponging on his friends or by false pretenses. Therefore he had chosen the park.

And all this was because an uncle had disinherited him, and cut down his allowance from liberality to nothing. And all that was because his nephew had disobeyed him concerning a certain girl, who comes not into this story — therefore, all readers who brush their hair toward its roots may be warned to read no further. There was another nephew, of a different branch, who had once been the prospective heir and favorite. Being without grace or hope, he had long ago disappeared in the mire. Now drag-nets were out for him; he was to be rehabilitated and restored. And so Vallance fell grandly as Lucifer to the lowest pit, joining the tattered ghosts in the little park.

Sitting there, he leaned far back on the hard bench and laughed a jet of cigarette smoke up to the lowest tree branches. The sudden severing of all his life's ties had brought him a free, thrilling, almost joyous elation. He felt precisely the sensation of the aëro-naut when he cuts loose his parachute and lets his balloon drift away.

The hour was nearly ten. Not many loungers were on the benches. The park-dweller, though a stubborn fighter against autumnal coolness, is slow to attack the advance line of spring's chilly cohorts.

Then arose one from a seat near the leaping foun-tain, and came and sat himself at Vallance's side. He was either young or old; cheap lodging-houses had flavored him mustily; razors and combs had passed him by; in him drink had been bottled and sealed in the devil's bond. He begged a match, which is the form of introduction among park benchers, and then he began to talk.

"You're not one of the regulars," he said to Vallance. "I know tailored clothes when I see 'em. You just stopped for a moment on your way through the park. Don't mind my talking to you for a while? I've got to be with somebody. I'm afraid — I'm afraid. I've told two or three of those bummers over there about it. They think I'm crazy. Say — let me tell you — all I've had to eat to-day was a couple of bretzels and an apple. To-morrow I'll stand in line to inherit three millions; and that restaurant you see over there with the autos around it will be too cheap for me to eat in. Don't believe it, do you?"

"Without the slightest trouble," said Vallance, with a laugh. "I lunched there yesterday. To-night I couldn't buy a five-cent cup of coffee."

"You don't look like one of us. Well, I guess those things happen. I used to be a high-flyer myself — some years ago. What knocked you out of the game?"

"I — oh, I lost my job," said Vallance.

"It's undiluted Hades, this city," went on the other. "One day you're eating from china; the next you are eating in China — a chop-suey joint. I've had more than my share of hard luck. For five years I've been little better than a panhandler. I was raised up to live expensively and do nothing. Say — I don't mind telling you — I've got to talk to somebody, you see, because I'm afraid — I'm afraid. My name's Ide. You wouldn't think that old Paulding, one of the millionaires on Riverside Drive, was my uncle, would you? Well, he is. I lived in his house once, and had all the money I wanted. Say, haven't you got the price of a couple of drinks about you — er — what's your name ——"

"Dawson," said Vallance. "No; I'm sorry to say that I'm all in, financially."

"I've been living for a week in a coal cellar on Division Street," went on Ide, "with a crook they called ' Blinky ' Morris. I didn't have anywhere else to go. While I was out to-day a chap with some papers in his pocket was there, asking for me. I didn't know but what he was a fly cop, so I didn't go around again till after dark. There was a letter there he had left for me. Say — Dawson, it was from a big downtown lawyer, Mead. I've seen his sign on Ann Street. Paulding wants me to play the prodigal nephew — wants me to come back and be his heir again and blow in his money. I'm to call at the lawyer's office at ten to-morrow and step into my old shoes again — heir to three million, Dawson, and $10,000 a year pocket money. And — I'm afraid — I'm afraid."

The vagrant leaped to his feet and raised both trembling arms above his head. He caught his breath and moaned hysterically.

Vallance seized his arm and forced him back to the bench.

"Be quiet!" he commanded, with something like disgust in his tones. "One would think you had lost a fortune, instead of being about to acquire one. Of what are you afraid?"

Ide cowered and shivered on the bench. He clung to Vallance's sleeve, and even in the dim glow of the Broadway lights the latest disinherited one could see drops on the other's brow wrung out by some strange terror.

"Why, I'm afraid something will happen to me before morning. I don't know what — something to keep me from coming into that money. I'm afraid a tree will fall on me — I'm afraid a cab will run over me, or a stone drop on me from a housetop, or something. I never was afraid before. I've sat in this park a hundred nights as calm as a graven image without knowing where my breakfast was to come from. But now it's different. I love money, Dawson — I'm happy as a god when it's trickling through my fingers, and people are bowing to me, with the music and the flowers and fine clothes all around. As long as I knew I was out of the game I didn't mind. I was even happy sitting here ragged and hungry, listening to the fountain jump and watching the carriages go up the avenue. But it's in reach of my hand again now — almost — and I can't stand it to wait twelve hours, Dawson — I can't stand it. There are fifty things that could happen to me — I could go blind — I might be attacked with heart disease — the world might come to an end before I could ——"

Ide sprang to his feet again, with a shriek. People stirred on the benches and began to look. Vallance took his arm.

" Come and walk," he said, soothingly. " And try to calm yourself. There is no need to become excited or alarmed. Nothing is going to happen to you. One night is like another."

" That's right," said Ide. " Stay with me, Dawson — that's a good fellow. Walk around with me awhile. I never went to pieces like this before, and I've had a good many hard knocks. Do you think you could hustle something in the way of a little lunch, old man? I'm afraid my nerve's too far gone to try any panhandling."

Vallance led his companion up almost deserted Fifth Avenue, and then westward along the Thirties toward Broadway. " Wait here a few minutes," he said, leaving Ide in a quiet and shadowed spot. He entered a familiar hotel, and strolled toward the bar quite in his old assured way.

" There's a poor devil outside, Jimmy," he said to the bartender, " who says he's hungry and looks it. You know what they do when you give them money. Fix up a sandwich or two for him; and I'll see that he doesn't throw it away."

" Certainly, Mr. Vallance," said the bartender. " They ain't all fakes. Don't like to see anybody go hungry."

He folded a liberal supply of the free lunch into a napkin. Vallance went with it and joined his companion. Ide pounced upon the food ravenously. " I haven't had any free lunch as good as this in a year," he said. " Aren't you going to eat any, Dawson? "

" I'm not hungry — thanks," said Vallance.

" We'll go back to the Square," said Ide. " The cops won't bother us there. I'll roll up the rest of this ham and stuff for our breakfast. I won't eat any more; I'm afraid I'll get sick. Suppose I'd die of cramps or something to-night, and never get to touch that money again! It's eleven hours yet till time to see that lawyer. You won't leave me, will you, Dawson? I'm afraid something might happen. You haven't any place to go, have you? "

" No," said Vallance, " nowhere to-night. I'll have a bench with you."

" You take it cool," said Ide, " if you've told it to me straight. I should think a man put on the bum from a good job just in one day would be tearing his hair."

" I believe I've already remarked," said Vallance, laughing, " that I would have thought that a man who was expecting to come into a fortune on the next day would be feeling pretty easy and quiet."

" It's funny business," philosophized Ide, " about the way people take things, anyhow. Here's your bench, Dawson, right next to mine. The light don't shine in your eyes here. Say, Dawson, I'll get the old man to give you a letter to somebody about a job when I get back home. You've helped me a lot to-night. I don't believe I could have gone through the night if I hadn't struck you."

" Thank you," said Vallance. " Do you lie down or sit up on these when you sleep? "

For hours Vallance gazed almost without winking at the stars through the branches of the trees and listened to the sharp slapping of horses' hoofs on the sea of asphalt to the south. His mind was active, but his feelings were dormant. Every emotion seemed to have been eradicated. He felt no regrets, no fears, no pain or discomfort. Even when he thought of the girl, it was as of an inhabitant of one of those remote stars at which he gazed. He remembered the absurd antics of his companion and laughed softly, yet without a feeling of mirth. Soon the daily army of milk wagons made of the city a

roaring drum to which they marched. Vallance fell
asleep on his comfortless bench.

At ten o'clock on the next day the two stood at the
door of Lawyer Mead's office in Ann Street.

Ide's nerves fluttered worse than ever when the
hour approached; and Vallance could not decide to
leave him a possible prey to the dangers he dreaded.

When they entered the office, Lawyer Mead looked
at them wonderingly. He and Vallance were old
friends. After his greeting, he turned to Ide, who
stood with white face and trembling limbs before the
expected crisis.

" I sent a second letter to your address last night,
Mr. Ide," he said.   " I learned this morning that
you were not there to receive it.   It will inform you
that Mr. Paulding has reconsidered his offer to take
you back into favor.   He has decided not to do so,
and desires you to understand that no change will be
made in the relations existing between you and
him."

Ide's trembling suddenly ceased. The color came
back to his face, and he straightened his back. His
jaw went forward half an inch, and a gleam came
into his eye. He pushed back his battered hat with
one hand, and extended the other, with levelled fingers, toward the lawyer. He took a long breath and
then laughed sardonically.

" Tell old Paulding he may go to the devil," he

said, loudly and clearly, and turned and walked out of the office with a firm and lively step.

Lawyer Mead turned on his heel to Vallance and smiled.

" I am glad you came in," he said, genially. " Your uncle wants you to return home at once. He is reconciled to the situation that led to his hasty action, and desires to say that all will be as ——"

" Hey, Adams! " cried Lawyer Mead, breaking his sentence, and calling to his clerk. " Bring a glass of water — Mr. Vallance has fainted."

THE PLUTONIAN FIRE

THERE are a few editor men with whom I am privileged to come in contact. It has not been long since it was their habit to come in contact with me. There is a difference.

They tell me that with a large number of the manuscripts that are submitted to them come advices (in the way of a boost) from the author asseverating that the incidents in the story are true. The destination of such contributions depends wholly upon the question of the inclosure of stamps. Some are returned, the rest are thrown on the floor in a corner on top of a pair of gum shoes, an overturned statuette of the Winged Victory, and a pile of old magazines containing a picture of the editor in the act of reading the latest copy of *Le Petit Journal*, right side up — you can tell by the illustrations. It is only a legend that there are waste baskets in editors' offices.

Thus is truth held in disrepute. But in time truth and science and nature will adapt themselves to art. Things will happen logically, and the villain be discomfited instead of being elected to the board of directors. But in the meantime fiction must not only be divorced from fact, but must pay alimony and be awarded custody of the press despatches.

This preamble is to warn you off the grade crossing of a true story. Being that, it shall be told simply, with conjunctions substituted for adjectives wherever possible, and whatever evidences of style may appear in it shall be due to the linotype man. It is a story of the literary life in a great city, and it should be of interest to every author within a 20-mile radius of Gosport, Ind., whose desk holds a MS. story beginning thus: " While the cheers following his nomination were still ringing through the old court-house, Harwood broke away from the congratulating handclasps of his henchmen and hurried to Judge Creswell's house to find Ida."

Pettit came up out of Alabama to write fiction. The Southern papers had printed eight of his stories under an editorial caption identifying the author as the son of " the gallant Major Pettingill Pettit, our former County Attorney and hero of the battle of Lookout Mountain."

Pettit was a rugged fellow, with a kind of shame-faced culture, and my good friend. His father kept a general store in a little town called Hosea. Pettit had been raised in the pine-woods and broom-sedge fields adjacent thereto. He had in his gripsack two manuscript novels of the adventures in Picardy of one Gaston Laboulaye, Vicompte de Montrepos, in

the year 1329. That's nothing. We all do that.
And some day when we make a hit with the little
sketch about a newsy and his lame dog, the editor
prints the other one for us — or " on us," as the saying is — and then — and then we have to get a big
valise and peddle those patent air-draft gas burners.
At $1.25 everybody should have 'em.

I took Pettit to the red-brick house which was to
appear in an article entitled " Literary Landmarks
of Old New York," some day when we got through
with it. He engaged a room there, drawing on the
general store for his expenses. I showed New York
to him, and he did not mention how much narrower
Broadway is than Lee Avenue in Hosea. This
seemed a good sign, so I put the final test.

" Suppose you try your hand at a descriptive article," I suggested, " giving your impressions of New
York as seen from the Brooklyn Bridge. The fresh
point of view, the ——"

" Don't be a fool," said Pettit. " Let's go have
some beer. On the whole I rather like the city."

We discovered and enjoyed the only true Bohemia.
Every day and night we repaired to one of those
palaces of marble and glass and tilework, where goes
on a tremendous and sounding epic of life. Valhalla
itself could not be more glorious and sonorous. The
classic marble on which we ate, the great, light-
flooded, vitreous front, adorned with snow-white

scrolls; the grand Wagnerian din of clanking cups
and bowls, the flashing staccato of brandishing cut-
lery, the piercing recitative of the white-aproned
grub-maidens at the morgue-like banquet tables; the
recurrent lied-motif of the cash-register — it was a
gigantic, triumphant welding of art and sound, a
deafening, soul-uplifting pageant of heroic and em-
blematic life. And the beans were only ten cents.
We wondered why our fellow-artists cared to dine at
sad little tables in their so-called Bohemian restaurants; and we shuddered lest they should seek out our
resorts and make them conspicuous with their presence.

Pettit wrote many stories, which the editors returned to him. He wrote love stories, a thing I have
always kept free from, holding the belief that the
well-known and popular sentiment is not properly a
matter for publication, but something to be privately
handled by the alienists and florists. But the editors
had told him that they wanted love stories, because
they said the women read them.

Now, the editors are wrong about that, of course.
Women do not read the love stories in the magazines.
They read the poker-game stories and the recipes
for cucumber lotion. The love stories are read by
fat cigar drummers and little ten-year-old girls. I
am not criticising the judgment of editors. They
are mostly very fine men, but a man can be but one

man, with individual opinions and tastes. I knew
two associate editors of a magazine who were wonderfully alike in almost everything. And yet one
of them was very fond of Flaubert, while the other
preferred gin.

Pettit brought me his returned manuscripts, and
we looked them over together to find out why they
were not accepted. They seemed to me pretty fair
stories, written in a good style, and ended, as they
should, at the bottom of the last page.

They were well constructed and the events were
marshalled in orderly and logical sequence. But I
thought I detected a lack of living substance — it
was much as if I gazed at a symmetrical array of
presentable clamshells from which the succulent and
vital inhabitants had been removed. I intimated that
the author might do well to get better acquainted with
his theme.

"You sold a story last week," said Pettit, "about
a gun fight in an Arizona mining town in which the
hero drew his Colt's .45 and shot seven bandits as
fast as they came in the door. Now, if a six-shooter
could ——"

"Oh, well," said I, "that's different. Arizona is
a long way from New York. I could have a man
stabbed with a lariat or chased by a pair of chap-
arreras if I wanted to, and it wouldn't be noticed
until the usual error-sharp from around McAdams

Junction isolates the erratum and writes in to the papers about it. But you are up against another proposition. This thing they call love is as common around New York as it is in Sheboygan during the young onion season. It may be mixed here with a little commercialism — they read Byron, but they look up Bradstreet's, too, while they're among the B's, and Brigham also if they have time — but it's pretty much the same old internal disturbance everywhere. You can fool an editor with a fake picture of a cowboy mounting a pony with his left hand on the saddle horn, but you can't put him up a tree with a love story. So, you've got to fall in love and then write the real thing."

Pettit did. I never knew whether he was taking my advice or whether he fell an accidental victim.

There was a girl he had met at one of these studio contrivances — a glorious, impudent, lucid, open-minded girl with hair the color of Culmbacher, and a good-natured way of despising you. She was a New York girl.

Well (as the narrative style permits us to say infrequently), Pettit went to pieces. All those pains, those lover's doubts, those heart-burnings and tremors of which he had written so unconvincingly were his. Talk about Shylock's pound of flesh! Twenty-five pounds Cupid got from Pettit. Which is the usurer?

One night Pettit came to my room exalted. Pale and haggard but exalted. She had given him a jonquil.

" Old Hoss," said he, with a new smile flickering around his mouth, " I believe I could write that story to-night — the one, you know, that is to win out. I can feel it. I don't know whether it will come out or not, but I can feel it."

I pushed him out of my door. " Go to your room and write it," I ordered. " Else I can see your finish. I told you this must come first. Write it to-night and put it under my door when it is done. Put it under my door to-night when it is finished — don't keep it until to-morrow."

I was reading my bully old pal Montaigne at two o'clock when I heard the sheets rustle under my door. I gathered them up and read the story.

The hissing of geese, the languishing cooing of doves, the braying of donkeys, the chatter of irresponsible sparrows — these were in my mind's ear as I read. " Suffering Sappho ! " I exclaimed to myself. " Is this the divine fire that is supposed to ignite genius and make it practicable and wage-earning ? "

The story was sentimental drivel, full of whimpering soft-heartedness and gushing egoism. All the art that Pettit had acquired was gone. A perusal of its buttery phrases would have made a cynic of a sighing chambermaid.

In the morning Pettit came to my room. I read him his doom mercilessly. He laughed idiotically.

" All right, Old Hoss," he said, cheerily, " make cigar-lighters of it. What's the difference? I'm going to take her to lunch at Claremont to-day."

There was about a month of it. And then Pettit came to me bearing an invisible mitten, with the fortitude of a dish-rag. He talked of the grave and South America and prussic acid; and I lost an afternoon getting him straight. I took him out and saw that large and curative doses of whiskey were administered to him. I warned you this was a true story —'ware your white ribbons if you follow this tale. For two weeks I fed him whiskey and Omar, and read to him regularly every evening the column in the evening paper that reveals the secrets of female beauty. I recommend the treatment.

After Pettit was cured he wrote more stories. He recovered his old-time facility and did work just short of good enough. Then the curtain rose on the third act.

A little, dark-eyed, silent girl from New Hampshire, who was studying applied design, fell deeply in love with him. She was the intense sort, but externally *glacé*, such as New England sometimes fools us with. Pettit liked her mildly, and took her about a good deal. She worshipped him, and now and then bored him.

There came a climax when she tried to jump out of a window, and he had to save her by some perfunctory, unmeant wooing. Even I was shaken by the depths of the absorbing affection she showed. Home, friends, traditions, creeds went up like thistle-down in the scale against her love. It was really discomposing.

One night again Pettit sauntered in, yawning. As he had told me before, he said he felt that he could do a great story, and as before I hunted him to his room and saw him open his inkstand. At one o'clock the sheets of paper slid under my door.

I read that story, and I jumped up, late as it was, with a whoop of joy. Old Pettit had done it. Just as though it lay there, red and bleeding, a woman's heart was written into the lines. You couldn't see the joining, but art, exquisite art, and pulsing nature had been combined into a love story that took you by the throat like the quinsy. I broke into Pettit's room and beat him on the back and called him names — names high up in the galaxy of the immortals that we admired. And Pettit yawned and begged to be allowed to sleep.

On the morrow, I dragged him to an editor. The great man read, and, rising, gave Pettit his hand. That was a decoration, a wreath of bay, and a guarantee of rent.

And then old Pettit smiled slowly. I call him Gentleman Pettit now to myself. It's a miserable name to give a man, but it sounds better than it looks in print.

"I see," said old Pettit, as he took up his story and began tearing it into small strips. "I see the game now. You can't write with ink, and you can't write with your own heart's blood, but you can write with the heart's blood of some one else. You have to be a cad before you can be an artist. Well, I am for old Alabam and the Major's store. Have you got a light, Old Hoss?"

I went with Pettit to the dépôt and died hard.

"Shakespeare's sonnets?" I blurted, making a last stand. "How about him?"

"A cad," said Pettit. "They give it to you, and you sell it — love, you know. I'd rather sell ploughs for father."

"But," I protested, "you are reversing the decision of the world's greatest ——"

"Good-by, Old Hoss," said Pettit.

"Critics," I continued. "But — say — if the Major can use a fairly good salesman and bookkeeper down there in the store, let me know, will you?"

NEMESIS AND THE CANDY MAN

WE sail at eight in the morning on the *Celtic*," said Honoria, plucking a loose thread from her lace sleeve.

"I heard so," said young Ives, dropping his hat, and muffing it as he tried to catch it, "and I came around to wish you a pleasant voyage."

"Of course you heard it," said Honoria, coldly sweet, "since we have had no opportunity of informing you ourselves."

Ives looked at her pleadingly, but with little hope.

Outside in the street a high-pitched voice chanted, not unmusically, a commercial gamut of "Cand-ee-ee-ee-s! Nice, fresh cand-ee-ee-ee-ees!"

"It's our old candy man," said Honoria, leaning out the window and beckoning. "I want some of his motto kisses. There's nothing in the Broadway shops half so good."

The candy man stopped his pushcart in front of the old Madison Avenue home. He had a holiday and festival air unusual to street peddlers. His tie was new and bright red, and a horseshoe pin, almost life-size, glittered speciously from its folds. His brown, thin face was crinkled into a semi-foolish

115

smile. Striped cuffs with dog-head buttons covered the tan on his wrists.

"I do believe he's going to get married," said Honoria, pityingly. "I never saw him taken that way before. And to-day is the first time in months that he has cried his wares, I am sure."

Ives threw a coin to the sidewalk. The candy man knows his customers. He filled a paper bag, climbed the old-fashioned stoop and handed it in.

"I remember ——" said Ives.

"Wait," said Honoria.

She took a small portfolio from the drawer of a writing desk and from the portfolio a slip of flimsy paper one-quarter of an inch by two inches in size.

"This," said Honoria, inflexibly, "was wrapped about the first one we opened."

"It was a year ago," apologized Ives, as he held out his hand for it,

> "As long as skies above are blue
> To you, my love, I will be true."

This he read from the slip of flimsy paper.

"We were to have sailed a fortnight ago," said Honoria, gossipingly. "It has been such a warm summer. The town is quite deserted. There is nowhere to go. Yet I am told that one or two of the roof gardens are amusing. The singing — and the dancing — on one or two seem to have met with approval."

Ives did not wince. When you are in the ring you are not surprised when your adversary taps you on the ribs.

" I followed the candy man that time," said Ives, irrelevantly, " and gave him five dollars at the corner of Broadway."

He reached for the paper bag in Honoria's lap, took out one of the square, wrapped confections and slowly unrolled it.

" Sara Chillingworth's father," said Honoria, " has given her an automobile."

" Read that," said Ives, handing over the slip that had been wrapped around the square of candy.

> "Life teaches us—how to live,
> Love teaches us—to forgive."

Honoria's cheeks turned pink.

" Honoria! " cried Ives, starting up from his chair.

" Miss Clinton," corrected Honoria, rising like Venus from the bead on the surf. " I warned you not to speak that name again."

" Honoria," repeated Ives, " you must hear me. I know I do not deserve your forgiveness, but I must have it. There is a madness that possesses one sometimes for which his better nature is not responsible.

I throw everything else but you to the winds. I strike off the chains that have bound me. I renounce the siren that lured me from you. Let the bought verse of that street peddler plead for me. It is you only whom I can love. Let your love forgive, and I swear to you that mine will be true ' as long as skies above are blue.' "

.   .   .   .   .   .

On the west side, between Sixth and Seventh Avenues, an alley cuts the block in the middle. It perishes in a little court in the centre of the block. The district is theatrical; the inhabitants, the bubbling froth of half a dozen nations. The atmosphere is Bohemian, the language polyglot, the locality precarious.

In the court at the rear of the alley lived the candy man. At seven o'clock he pushed his cart into the narrow entrance, rested it upon the irregular stone slats and sat upon one of the handles to cool himself. There was a great draught of cool wind through the alley.

There was a window above the spot where he always stopped his pushcart. In the cool of the afternoon, Mlle. Adèle, drawing card of the Aërial Roof Garden, sat at the window and took the air. Generally her ponderous mass of dark auburn hair was down, that the breeze might have the felicity of aiding Sidonie, the maid, in drying and airing it.

About her shoulders — the point of her that the photographers always made the most of — was loosely draped a heliotrope scarf. Her arms to the elbow were bare — there were no sculptors there to rave over them — but even the stolid bricks in the walls of the alley should not have been so insensate as to disapprove. While she sat thus Félice, another maid, anointed and bathed the small feet that twinkled and so charmed the nightly Aërial audiences.

Gradually Mademoiselle began to notice the candy man stopping to mop his brow and cool himself beneath her window. In the hands of her maids she was deprived for the time of her vocation — the charming and binding to her chariot of man. To lose time was displeasing to Mademoiselle. Here was the candy man — no fit game for her darts, truly — but of the sex upon which she had been born to make war.

After casting upon him looks of unseeing coldness for a dozen times, one afternoon she suddenly thawed and poured down upon him a smile that put to shame the sweets upon his cart.

"Candy man," she said, cooingly, while Sidonie followed her impulsive dive, brushing the heavy auburn hair, "don't you think I am beautiful?"

The candy man laughed harshly, and looked up, with his thin jaw set, while he wiped his forehead with a red-and-blue handkerchief.

" Yer'd make a dandy magazine cover," he said, grudgingly. " Beautiful or not is for them that cares. It's not my line. If yer lookin' for bouquets apply elsewhere between nine and twelve. I think we'll have rain."

Truly, fascinating a candy man is like killing rabbits in a deep snow; but the hunter's blood is widely diffused. Mademoiselle tugged a great coil of hair from Sidonie's hands and let it fall out the window.

" Candy man, have you a sweetheart anywhere with hair as long and soft as that? And with an arm so round? " She flexed an arm like Galatea's after the miracle across the window-sill.

The candy man cackled shrilly as he arranged a stock of butter-scotch that had tumbled down.

" Smoke up! " said he, vulgarly. " Nothin' doin' in the complimentary line. I'm too wise to be bamboozled by a switch of hair and a newly massaged arm. Oh, I guess you'll make good in the calcium, all right, with plenty of powder and paint on and the orchestra playing ' Under the Old Apple Tree.' But don't put on your hat and chase downstairs to fly to the Little Church Around the Corner with me. I've been up against peroxide and make-up boxes before. Say, all joking aside — don't you think we'll have rain? "

" Candy man," said Mademoiselle, softly, with her

lips curving and her chin dimpling, " don't you think I'm pretty? "

The candy man grinned.

" Savin' money, ain't yer? " said he, " by bein' yer own press agent. I smoke, but I haven't seen yer mug on any of the five-cent cigar boxes. It'd take a new brand of woman to get me goin', anyway. I know 'em from sidecombs to shoelaces. Gimme a good day's sales and steak-and-onions at seven and a pipe and an evenin' paper back there in the court, and I'll not trouble Lillian Russell herself to wink at me, if you please."

Mademoiselle pouted.

" Candy man," she said, softly and deeply, " yet you shall say that I am beautiful. All men say so and so shall you."

The candy man laughed and pulled out his pipe.

" Well," said he, " I must be goin' in. There is a story in the evenin' paper that I am readin'. Men are divin' in the seas for a treasure, and pirates are watchin' them from behind a reef. And there ain't a woman on land or water or in the air. Good-evenin'." And he trundled his pushcart down the alley and back to the musty court where he lived.

Incredibly to him who has not learned woman, Mademoiselle sat at the window each day and spread her nets for the ignominious game. Once she kept a grand cavalier waiting in her reception chamber for half an hour while she battered in vain the candy man's tough philosophy. His rough laugh chafed her vanity to its core. Daily he sat on his cart in the breeze of the alley while her hair was being ministered to, and daily the shafts of her beauty rebounded from his dull bosom pointless and ineffectual. Unworthy pique brightened her eyes. Pride-hurt she glowed upon him in a way that would have sent her higher adorers into an egoistic paradise. The candy man's hard eyes looked upon her with a half-concealed derision that urged her to the use of the sharpest arrow in her beauty's quiver.

One afternoon she leaned far over the sill, and she did not challenge and torment him as usual.

"Candy man," said she, "stand up and look into my eyes."

He stood up and looked into her eyes, with his harsh laugh like the sawing of wood. He took out his pipe, fumbled with it, and put it back into his pocket with a trembling hand.

"That will do," said Mademoiselle, with a slow smile. "I must go now to my *masseuse*. Good-evening."

The next evening at seven the candy man came and rested his cart under the window. But was it the candy man? His clothes were a bright new check. His necktie was a flaming red, adorned by a glittering horseshoe pin, almost life-size. His shoes were polished; the tan of his cheeks had paled — his hands had been washed. The window was empty, and he waited under it with his nose upward, like a hound hoping for a bone.

Mademoiselle came, with Sidonie carrying her load of hair. She looked at the candy man and smiled a slow smile that faded away into ennui. Instantly she knew that the game was bagged; and so quickly she wearied of the chase. She began to talk to Sidonie.

"Been a fine day," said the candy man, hollowly. "First time in a month I've felt first-class. Hit it up down old Madison, hollering out like I useter. Think it'll rain to-morrow?"

Mademoiselle laid two round arms on the cushion on the window-sill, and a dimpled chin upon them.

"Candy man," said she, softly, "do you not love me?"

The candy man stood up and leaned against the brick wall.

"Lady," said he, chokingly, "I've got $800 saved up. Did I say you wasn't beautiful? Take it every bit of it and buy a collar for your dog with it."

A sound as of a hundred silvery bells tinkled in the room of Mademoiselle. The laughter filled the alley and trickled back into the court, as strange a thing to enter there as sunlight itself. Mademoiselle was amused. Sidonie, a wise echo, added a sepulchral but faithful contralto. The laughter of the two seemed at last to penetrate the candy man. He fumbled with his horseshoe pin. At length Mademoiselle, exhausted, turned her flushed, beautiful face to the window.

"Candy man," said she, "go away. When I laugh Sidonie pulls my hair. I can but laugh while you remain there."

"Here is a note for Mademoiselle," said Félice, coming to the window in the room.

"There is no justice," said the candy man, lifting the handle of his cart and moving away.

Three yards he moved, and stopped. Loud shriek after shriek came from the window of Mademoiselle. Quickly he ran back. He heard a body thumping upon the floor and a sound as though heels beat alternately upon it.

"What is it?" he called.

Sidonie's severe head came into the window.

"Mademoiselle is overcome by bad news," she said. "One whom she loved with all her soul has gone — you may have heard of him — he is Monsieur Ives. He sails across the ocean to-morrow. Oh, you men!"

SQUARING THE CIRCLE

AT the hazard of wearying you this tale of vehement emotions must be prefaced by a discourse on geometry.

Nature moves in circles; Art in straight lines. The natural is rounded; the artificial is made up of angles. A man lost in the snow wanders, in spite of himself, in perfect circles; the city man's feet, denaturalized by rectangular streets and floors, carry him ever away from himself.

The round eyes of childhood typify innocence; the narrowed line of the flirt's optic proves the invasion of art. The horizontal mouth is the mark of determined cunning; who has not read Nature's most spontaneous lyric in lips rounded for the candid kiss?

Beauty is Nature in perfection; circularity is its chief attribute. Behold the full moon, the enchanting golf ball, the domes of splendid temples, the huckleberry pie, the wedding ring, the circus ring, the ring for the waiter, and the " round " of drinks.

On the other hand, straight lines show that Nature has been deflected. Imagine Venus's girdle transformed into a " straight front " !

When we begin to move in straight lines and turn

sharp corners our natures begin to change. The
consequence is that Nature, being more adaptive than
Art, tries to conform to its sterner regulations. The
result is often a rather curious product — for instance: A prize chrysanthemum, wood alcohol whiskey, a Republican Missouri, cauliflower *au gratin*,
and a New Yorker.

Nature is lost quickest in a big city. The cause
is geometrical, not moral. The straight lines of its
streets and architecture, the rectangularity of its
laws and social customs, the undeviating pavements,
the hard, severe, depressing, uncompromising rules
of all its ways — even of its recreation and sports —
coldly exhibit a sneering defiance of the curved line
of Nature.

Wherefore, it may be said that the big city has
demonstrated the problem of squaring the circle.
And it may be added that this mathematical introduction precedes an account of the fate of a Kentucky
feud that was imported to the city that has a habit
of making its importations conform to its angles.

The feud began in the Cumberland Mountains between the Folwell and the Harkness families. The
first victim of the homespun vendetta was a 'possum
dog belonging to Bill Harkness. The Harkness
family evened up this dire loss by laying out the
chief of the Folwell clan. The Folwells were prompt
at repartee. They oiled up their squirrel rifles and

made it feasible for Bill Harkness to follow his dog
to a land where the 'possums come down when treed
without the stroke of an ax.

The feud flourished for forty years. Harknesses
were shot at the plough, through their lamp-lit cabin
windows, coming from camp-meeting, asleep, in duello,
sober and otherwise, singly and in family groups,
prepared and unprepared. Folwells had the
branches of their family tree lopped off in similar
ways, as the traditions of their country prescribed
and authorized.

By and by the pruning left but a single member
of each family. And then Cal Harkness, probably
reasoning that further pursuance of the controversy
would give a too decided personal flavor to the feud,
suddenly disappeared from the relieved Cumberlands,
baulking the avenging hand of Sam, the ultimate op-
posing Folwell.

A year afterward Sam Folwell learned that his
hereditary, unsuppressed enemy was living in New
York City. Sam turned over the big iron wash-pot
in the yard, scraped off some of the soot, which he
mixed with lard and shined his boots with the compound. He put on his store clothes of butternut
dyed black, a white shirt and collar, and packed a
carpet-sack with Spartan *lingerie*. He took his
squirrel rifle from its hooks, but put it back again
with a sigh. However ethical and plausible the habit

might be in the Cumberlands, perhaps New York
would not swallow his pose of hunting squirrels among
the skyscrapers along Broadway. An ancient but
reliable Colt's revolver that he resurrected from a
bureau drawer seemed to proclaim itself the pink of
weapons for metropolitan adventure and vengeance.
This and a hunting-knife in a leather sheath, Sam
packed in the carpet-sack. As he started, muleback,
for the lowland railroad station the last Folwell
turned in his saddle and looked grimly at the little
cluster of white-pine slabs in the clump of cedars that
marked the Folwell burying-ground.

Sam Folwell arrived in New York in the night.
Still moving and living in the free circles of nature,
he did not perceive the formidable, pitiless, restless,
fierce angles of the great city waiting in the dark
to close about the rotundity of his heart and brain
and mould him to the form of its millions of re-shaped
victims. A cabby picked him out of the whirl, as
Sam himself had often picked a nut from a bed of
wind-tossed autumn leaves, and whisked him away
to a hotel commensurate to his boots and carpet-
sack.

On the next morning the last of the Folwells made
his sortie into the city that sheltered the last Harkness. The Colt was thrust beneath his coat and secured by a narrow leather belt; the hunting-knife
hung between his shoulder-blades, with the haft an

inch below his coat colar. He knew this much —
that Cal Harkness drove an express wagon somewhere in that town, and that he, Sam Folwell, had
come to kill him. And as he stepped upon the sidewalk the red came into his eye and the feud-hate into
his heart.

The clamor of the central avenues drew him thith-
erward. He had half expected to see Cal coming
down the street in his shirt-sleeves, with a jug and
a whip in his hand, just as he would have seen him
in Frankfort or Laurel City. But an hour went by
and Cal did not appear. Perhaps he was waiting in
ambush, to shoot him from a door or a window. Sam
kept a sharp eye on doors and windows for a while.

About noon the city tired of playing with its mouse
and suddenly squeezed him with its straight lines.

Sam Folwell stood where two great, rectangular
arteries of the city cross. He looked four ways, and
saw the world hurled from its orbit and reduced
by spirit level and tape to an edged and cornered
plane. All life moved on tracks, in grooves, according to system, within boundaries, by rote. The root
of life was the cube root; the measure of existence
was square measure. People streamed by in straight
rows; the horrible din and crash stupefied him.

Sam leaned against the sharp corner of a stone
building. Those faces passed him by thousands, and
none of them were turned toward him. A sudden fool-

ish fear that he had died and was a spirit, and that they could not see him, seized him. And then the city smote him with loneliness.

A fat man dropped out of the stream and stood a few feet distant, waiting for his car. Sam crept to his side and shouted above the tumult into his ear:

"The Rankinses' hogs weighed more'n ourn a whole passel, but the mast in thar neighborhood was a fine chance better than what it was down ——"

The fat man moved away unostentatiously, and bought roasted chestnuts to cover his alarm.

Sam felt the need of a drop of mountain dew. Across the street men passed in and out through swinging doors. Brief glimpses could be had of a glistening bar and its bedeckings. The feudist crossed and essayed to enter. Again had Art eliminated the familiar circle. Sam's hand found no door-knob — it slid, in vain, over a rectangular brass plate and polished oak with nothing even so large as a pin's head upon which his fingers might close.

Abashed, reddened, heartbroken, he walked away from the bootless door and sat upon a step. A locust club tickled him in the ribs.

"Take a walk for yourself," said the policeman. "You've been loafing around here long enough."

At the next corner a shrill whistle sounded in Sam's ear. He wheeled around and saw a black-browed vil-

lain scowling at him over peanuts heaped on a steam-
ing machine. He started across the street. An immense engine, running without mules, with the voice of
a bull and the smell of a smoky lamp, whizzed past,
grazing his knee. A cab-driver bumped him with a
hub and explained to him that kind words were in-
vented to be used on other occasions. A motorman
clanged his bell wildly and, for once in his life, cor-
roborated a cab-driver. A large lady in a changeable
silk waist dug an elbow into his back, and a newsy
pensively pelted him with banana rinds, murmuring,
" I hates to do it — but if anybody seen me let it
pass! "

Cal Harkness, his day's work over and his express
wagon stabled, turned the sharp edge of the building that, by the cheek of architects, is modelled upon
a safety razor. Out of the mass of hurrying people
his eye picked up, three yards away, the surviving
bloody and implacable foe of his kith and kin.

He stopped short and wavered for a moment, being unarmed and sharply surprised. But the keen
mountaineer's eye of Sam Folwell had picked him out.

There was a sudden spring, a ripple in the stream
of passers-by and the sound of Sam's voice crying:

" Howdy, Cal! I'm durned glad to see ye."

And in the angles of Broadway, Fifth Avenue and
Twenty-third Street the Cumberland feudists shook
hands.

ROSES, RUSES AND ROMANCE

RAVENEL — Ravenel, the traveller, artist and poet, threw his magazine to the floor. Sammy Brown, broker's clerk, who sat by the window, jumped.

"What is it, Ravvy?" he asked. "The critics been hammering your stock down?"

"Romance is dead," said Ravenel, lightly. When Ravenel spoke lightly he was generally serious. He picked up the magazine and fluttered its leaves.

"Even a Philistine, like you, Sammy," said Ravenel, seriously (a tone that insured him to be speaking lightly), "ought to understand. Now, here is a magazine that once printed Poe and Lowell and Whitman and Bret Harte and Du Maurier and Lanier and — well, that gives you the idea. The current number has this literary feast to set before you: an article on the stokers and coal bunkers of battle-ships, an exposé of the methods employed in making liverwurst, a continued story of a Standard Preferred International Baking Powder deal in Wall Street, a 'poem' on the bear that the President missed, another 'story' by a young woman who spent a week as a spy making overalls on the East Side, another 'fiction' story that reeks of the 'garage' and a cer-

tain make of automobile. Of course, the title contains
the words ' Cupid ' and ' Chauffeur '— an article on
naval strategy, illustrated with cuts of the Spanish
Armada, and the new Staten Island ferry-boats; another story of a political boss who won the love of a
Fifth Avenue belle by blackening her eye and refusing
to vote for an iniquitous ordinance (it doesn't say
whether it was in the Street-Cleaning Department or
Congress), and nineteen pages by the editors brag-
ging about the circulation. The whole thing, Sammy,
is an obituary on Romance."

Sammy Brown sat comfortably in the leather arm-
chair by the open window. His suit was a vehement
brown with visible checks, beautifully matched in
shade by the ends of four cigars that his vest pocket
poorly concealed. Light tan were his shoes, gray his
socks, sky-blue his apparent linen, snowy and high
and adamantine his collar, against which a black butterfly had alighted and spread his wings. Sammy's
face — least important — was round and pleasant
and pinkish, and in his eyes you saw no haven for
fleeing Romance.

That window of Ravenel's apartment opened upon
an old garden full of ancient trees and shrubbery.
The apartment-house towered above one side of it;
a high brick wall fended it from the street; opposite Ravenel's window an old, old mansion stood, half-
hidden in the shade of the summer foliage. The house

was a castle besieged. The city howled and roared
and shrieked and beat upon its double doors, and
shook white, fluttering checks above the wall, offering
terms of surrender. The gray dust settled upon the
trees; the siege was pressed hotter, but the draw-
bridge was not lowered. No further will the language
of chivalry serve. Inside lived an old gentleman who
loved his home and did not wish to sell it. That is
all the romance of the besieged castle.

Three or four times every week came Sammy
Brown to Ravenel's apartment. He belonged to the
poet's club, for the former Browns had been conspicuous, though Sammy had been vulgarized by
Business. He had no tears for departed Romance.
The song of the ticker was the one that reached
his heart, and when it came to matters equine and
batting scores he was something of a pink edition.
He loved to sit in the leather armchair by Ravenel's
window. And Ravenel didn't mind particularly.
Sammy seemed to enjoy his talk; and then the broker's
clerk was such a perfect embodiment of modernity and
the day's sordid practicality that Ravenel rather
liked to use him as a scapegoat.

" I'll tell you what's the matter with you," said
Sammy, with the shrewdness that business had taught
him. " The magazine has turned down some of your
poetry stunts. That's why you are sore at it."

" That would be a good guess in Wall Street or in

a campaign for the presidency of a woman's club,"
said Ravenel, quietly. "Now, there is a poem — if
you will allow me to call it that — of my own in this
number of the magazine."

"Read it to me," said Sammy, watching a cloud
of pipe-smoke he had just blown out the window.

Ravenel was no greater than Achilles. No one is.
There is bound to be a spot. The Somebody-or-Other
must take hold of us somewhere when she dips us in
the Something-or-Other that makes us invulnerable.
He read aloud this verse in the magazine:

THE FOUR ROSES

"One rose I twined within your hair—
   (White rose, that spake of worth);
And one you placed upon your breast—
   (Red rose, love's seal of birth).
You plucked another from its stem—
   (Tea rose, that means for aye);
And one you gave—that bore for me
   The thorns of memory."

"That's a crackerjack," said Sammy, admiringly.

"There are five more verses," said Ravenel, patiently sardonic. "One naturally pauses at the end
of each. Of course ——"

"Oh, let's have the rest, old man," shouted Sammy,
contritely, "I didn't mean to cut you off. I'm not
much of a poetry expert, you know. I never saw a
poem that didn't look like it ought to have terminal

facilities at the end of every verse. Reel off the rest of it."

Ravenel sighed, and laid the magazine down. " All right," said Sammy, cheerfully, " we'll have it next time. I'll be off now. Got a date at five o'clock."

He took a last look at the shaded green garden and left, whistling in an off key an untuneful air from a roofless farce comedy.

The next afternoon Ravenel, while polishing a ragged line of a new sonnet, reclined by the window overlooking the besieged garden of the unmercenary baron. Suddenly he sat up, spilling two rhymes and a syllable or two..

Through the trees one window of the old mansion could be seen clearly. In its window, draped in flowing white, leaned the angel of all his dreams of romance and poesy. Young, fresh as a drop of dew, graceful as a spray of clematis, conferring upon the garden hemmed in by the roaring traffic the air of a princess's bower, beautiful as any flower sung by poet — thus Ravenel saw her for the first time. She lingered for a while, and then disappeared within, leaving a few notes of a birdlike ripple of song to reach his entranced ears through the rattle of cabs and the snarling of the electric cars.

Thus, as if to challenge the poet's flaunt at romance and to punish him for his recreancy to the undying spirit of youth and beauty, this vision had

dawned upon him with a thrilling and accusive power.
And so metabolic was the power that in an instant
the atoms of Ravenel's entire world were redistrib-
uted. The laden drays that passed the house in which
she lived rumbled a deep double-bass to the tune of
love. The newsboys' shouts were the notes of singing
birds; that garden was the pleasance of the Capulets;
the janitor was an ogre; himself a knight, ready with
sword, lance or lute.

Thus does romance show herself amid forests of
brick and stone when she gets lost in the city, and
there has to be sent out a general alarm to find her
again.

At four in the afternoon Ravenel looked out across
the garden. In the window of his hopes were set
four small vases, each containing a great, full-blown
rose — red and white. And, as he gazed, she leaned
above them, shaming them with her loveliness and
seeming to direct her eyes pensively toward his own
window. And then, as though she had caught his
respectful but ardent regard, she melted away, leaving
the fragrant emblems on the window-sill.

" Yes, emblems! — he would be unworthy if he had
not understood. She had read his poem, " The Four
Roses "; it had reached her heart; and this was its
romantic answer. Of course she must know that
Ravenel, the poet, lived there across her garden. His
picture, too, she must have seen in the magazines.

The delicate, tender, modest, flattering message could not be ignored.

Ravenel noticed beside the roses a small flowering-pot containing a plant. Without shame he brought his opera-glasses and employed them from the cover of his window-curtain. A nutmeg geranium!

With the true poetic instinct he dragged a book of useless information from his shelves, and tore open the leaves at " The Language of Flowers."

" Geranium, Nutmeg — I expect a meeting."

So! Romance never does things by halves. If she comes back to you she brings gifts and her knitting, and will sit in your chimney-corner if you will let her.

And now Ravenel smiled. The lover smiles when he thinks he has won. The woman who loves ceases to smile with victory. He ends a battle; she begins hers. What a pretty idea to set the four roses in her window for him to see! She must have a sweet, poetic soul. And now to contrive the meeting.

A whistling and slamming of doors preluded the coming of Sammy Brown.

Ravenel smiled again. Even Sammy Brown was shone upon by the far-flung rays of the renaissance. Sammy, with his ultra clothes, his horseshoe pin, his plump face, his trite slang, his uncomprehending admiration of Ravenel — the broker's clerk made an excellent foil to the new, bright unseen visitor to the poet's sombre apartment.

Sammy went to his old seat by the window, and looked out over the dusty green foliage in the garden. Then he looked at his watch, and rose hastily.

" By grabs! " he exclaimed. " Twenty after four! I can't stay, old man; I've got a date at 4:30."

" Why did you come, then? " asked Ravenel, with sarcastic jocularity, " if you had an engagement at that time. I thought you business men kept better account of your minutes and seconds than that."

Sammy hesitated in the doorway and turned pinker.

" Fact is, Ravvy," he explained, as to a customer whose margin is exhausted, " I didn't know I had it till I came. I'll tell you, old man — there's a dandy girl in that old house next door that I'm dead gone on. I put it straight — we're engaged. The old man says ' nit '— but that don't go. He keeps her pretty close. I can see Edith's window from yours here. She gives me a tip when she's going shopping, and I meet her. It's 4:30 to-day. Maybe I ought to have explained sooner, but I know it's all right with you — so long."

" How do you get your ' tip,' as you call it? " asked Ravenel, losing a little spontaneity from his smile.

" Roses," said Sammy, briefly. " Four of 'em to-

day.   Means four o'clock at the corner of Broadway
and Twenty-third."

"But the geranium?" persisted Ravenel, clutch-
ing at the end of flying Romance's trailing robe.

"Means half-past," shouted Sammy from the hall.
"See you to-morrow."

THE CITY OF DREADFUL NIGHT

DURING the recent warmed-over spell," said my friend Carney, driver of express wagon No. 8,606, " a good many opportunities was had of observing human nature through peekaboo waists.

" The Park Commissioner and the Commissioner of Polis and the Forestry Commission gets together and agrees to let the people sleep in the parks until the Weather Bureau gets the thermometer down again to a living basis. So they draws up open-air resolutions and has them O. K.'d by the Secretary of Agriculture, Mr. Comstock and the Village Improvement Mosquito Exterminating Society of South Orange, N. J.

" When the proclamation was made opening up to the people by special grant the public parks that belong to 'em, there was a general exodus into Central Park by the communities existing along its borders. In ten minutes after sundown you'd have thought that there was an undress rehearsal of a potato famine in Ireland and a Kishineff massacre. They come by families, gangs, clambake societies, clans, clubs and tribes from all sides to enjoy a cool sleep on the grass. Them that didn't have oil stoves brought along plenty of blankets, so as not to be upset with the cold and discomforts of sleeping outdoors. By building fires of the shade trees and huddling together in the bridle paths, and burrowing under the grass where the ground was soft enough, the likes of 5,000 head of people successfully battled against the night air in Central Park alone.

"Ye know I live in the elegant furnished apartment house called the Beersheba Flats, over against the elevated portion of the New York Central Railroad.

"When the order come to the flats that all hands must turn out and sleep in the park, according to the instructions of the consulting committee of the City Club and the Murphy Draying, Returfing and Sodding Company, there was a look of a couple of fires and an eviction all over the place.

"The tenants began to pack up feather beds, rubber boots, strings of garlic, hot-water bags, portable canoes and scuttles of coal to take along for the sake of comfort. The sidewalk looked like a Russian camp in Oyama's line of march. There was wailing and lamenting up and down stairs from Danny Geoghegan's flat on the top floor to the apartments of Missis Goldsteinupski on the first.

"'For why,' says Danny, coming down and raging in his blue yarn socks to the janitor, 'should I be turned out of me comfortable apartmints to lay in the dirty grass like a rabbit? 'Tis like Jerome to

stir up trouble wid small matters like this instead
of ——"

" 'Whist!' says Officer Reagan on the sidewalk,
rapping with his club. ' 'Tis not Jerome. 'Tis by
order of the Polis Commissioner. Turn out every
one of yez and hike yerselves to the park.'

" Now, 'twas a peaceful and happy home that all
of us had in them same Beersheba Flats. The
O'Dowds and the Steinowitzes and the Callahans and
the Cohens and the Spizzinellis and the McManuses
and the Spiegelmayers and the Joneses — all nations
of us, we lived like one big family together. And
when the hot nights come along we kept a line of
childher reaching from the front door to Kelly's on the
corner, passing along the cans of beer from one to
another without the trouble of running after it. And
with no more clothing on than is provided for in the
statutes, sitting in all the windies, with a cool growler
in every one, and your feet out in the air, and the
Rosenstein girls singing on the fire-escape of the sixth
floor, and Patsy Rourke's flute going in the eighth,
and the ladies calling each other synonyms out the windies, and now and then a breeze sailing in over Mister
Depew's Central — I tell you the Beersheba Flats was
a summer resort that made the Catskills look like
a hole in the ground. With his person full of beer
and his feet out the windy and his old woman frying
pork chops over a charcoal furnace and the childher

dancing in cotton slips on the sidewalk around the organ-grinder and the rent paid for a week — what does a man want better on a hot night than that? And then comes this ruling of the polis driving people out o' their comfortable homes to sleep in parks — 'twas for all the world like a ukase of them Russians —'twill be heard from again at next election time.

"Well, then, Officer Reagan drives the whole lot of us to the park and turns us in by the nearest gate. 'Tis dark under the trees, and all the childher sets up to howling that they want to go home.

"'Ye'll pass the night in this stretch of woods and scenery,' says Officer Reagan. ''Twill be fine and imprisonment for insoolting the Park Commissioner and the Chief of the Weather Bureau if ye refuse. I'm in charge of thirty acres between here and the Agyptian Monument, and I advise ye to give no trouble. 'Tis sleeping on the grass yez all have been condemned to by the authorities. Yez'll be permitted to leave in the morning, but ye must retoorn be night. Me orders was silent on the subject of bail, but I'll find out if 'tis required and there'll be bondsmen at the gate.'

"There being no lights except along the automobile drives, us 179 tenants of the Beersheba Flats prepared to spend the night as best we could in the raging forest. Them that brought blankets and kin-

dling wood was best off. They got fires started and
wrapped the blankets round their heads and laid
down, cursing, in the grass. There was nothing to
see, nothing to drink, nothing to do. In the dark we
had no way of telling friend or foe except by feeling
the noses of 'em. I brought along me last winter
overcoat, me tooth-brush, some quinine pills and the
red quilt off the bed in me flat. Three times during
the night somebody rolled on me quilt and stuck his
knees against the Adam's apple of me. And three
times I judged his character by running me hand over
his face, and three times I rose up and kicked the in-
truder down the hill to the gravelly walk below. And
then some one with a flavor of Kelly's whiskey snug-
gled up to me, and I found his nose turned up the
right way, and I says: ' Is that you, then, Patsey? '
and he says, ' It is, Carney. How long do you think
it'll last? '

" ' I'm no weather-prophet,' says I, ' but if they
bring out a strong anti-Tammany ticket next fall it
ought to get us home in time to sleep on a bed once
or twice before they line us up at the polls.'

" ' A-playing of my flute into the airshaft,' says
Patsey Rourke, ' and a-perspiring in me own windy
to the joyful noise of the passing trains and the smell
of liver and onions and a-reading of the latest murder in the smoke of the cooking is well enough for
me,' says he. ' What is this herding us in grass for,

not to mention the crawling things with legs that walk up the trousers of us, and the Jersey snipes that peck at us, masquerading under the name and denomination of mosquitoes. What is it all for Carney, and the rint going on just the same over at the flats?'

"'Tis the great annual Municipal Free Night Outing Lawn Party,' says I, 'given by the polis, Hetty Green and the Drug Trust. During the heated season they hold a week of it in the principal parks. 'Tis a scheme to reach that portion of the people that's not worth taking up to North Beach for a fish fry.'

"'I can't sleep on the ground,' says Patsey, 'wid any benefit. I have the hay fever and the rheumatism, and me ear is full of ants.'

"Well, the night goes on, and the ex-tenants of the Flats groans and stumbles around in the dark, trying to find rest and recreation in the forest. The childher is screaming with the coldness, and the janitor makes hot tea for 'em and keeps the fires going with the signboards that point to the Tavern and the Casino. The tenants try to lay down on the grass by families in the dark, but you're lucky if you can sleep next to a man from the same floor or believing in the same religion. Now and then a Murphy, accidental, rolls over on the grass of a Rosenstein, or a Cohen tries to crawl under the O'Grady bush, and then there's a feeling of noses and somebody is rolled down the hill to the driveway and stays there. There is some hair-pulling among the women folks, and everybody spanks the nearest howling kid to him by the sense of feeling only, regardless of its parentage and ownership. 'Tis hard to keep up the social distinctions in the dark that flourish by daylight in the Beersheba Flats. Mrs. Rafferty, that despises the asphalt that a Dago treads on, wakes up in the morning with her feet in the bosom of Antonio Spizzinelli. And Mike O'Dowd, that always threw peddlers downstairs as fast as he came upon 'em, has to unwind old Isaacstein's whiskers from around his neck, and wake up the whole gang at daylight. But here and there some few got acquainted and overlooked the discomforts of the elements. There was five engagements to be married announced at the flats the next morning.

"About midnight I gets up and wrings the dew out of my hair, and goes to the side of the driveway and sits down. At one side of the park I could see the lights in the streets and houses; and I was thinking how happy them folks was who could chase the duck and smoke their pipes at their windows, and keep cool and pleasant like nature intended for 'em to.

"Just then an automobile stops by me, and a fine-looking, well-dressed man steps out.

"' Me man,' says he, ' can you tell me why all these people are lying around on the grass in the park? I thought it was against the rules.'

"'Twas an ordinance,' says I, 'just passed by the Polis Department and ratified by the Turf Cutters' Association, providing that all persons not carrying a license number on their rear axles shall keep in the public parks until further notice. Fortunately, the orders comes this year during a spell of fine weather, and the mortality, except on the borders of the lake and along the automobile drives, will not be any greater than usual.'

"'Who are these people on the side of the hill?' asks the man.

"'Sure,' says I, 'none others than the tenants of the Beersheba Flats — a fine home for any man, especially on hot nights. May daylight come soon!'

"'They come here be night,' says he, 'and breathe in the pure air and the fragrance of the flowers and trees. They do that,' says he, 'coming every night from the burning heat of dwellings of brick and stone.'

"'And wood,' says I. 'And marble and plaster and iron.'

"'The matter will be attended to at once,' says the man, putting up his book.

"'Are ye the Park Commissioner?' I asks.

"'I own the Beersheba Flats,' says he. 'God bless the grass and the trees that give extra benefits to a man's tenants. The rents shall be raised fifteen per cent. to-morrow. Good-night,' says he."

THE EASTER OF THE SOUL

IT is hardly likely that a goddess may die. Then Eastre, the old Saxon goddess of spring, must be laughing in her muslin sleeve at people who believe that Easter, her namesake, exists only along certain strips of Fifth Avenue pavement after church service.

Aye! It belongs to the world. The ptarmigan in Chilkoot Pass discards his winter white feathers for brown; the Patagonian Beau Brummell oils his chignon and clubs him another sweetheart to drag to his skull-strewn flat. And down in Chrystie Street ——

Mr. "Tiger" McQuirk arose with a feeling of disquiet that he did not understand. With a practised foot he rolled three of his younger brothers like logs out of his way as they lay sleeping on the floor. Before a foot-square looking glass hung by the window he stood and shaved himself. If that may seem to you a task too slight to be thus impressively chronicled, I bear with you; you do not know of the areas to be accomplished in traversing the cheek and chin of Mr. McQuirk.

McQuirk, senior, had gone to work long before. The big son of the house was idle. He was a marble-cutter, and the marble-cutters were out on a strike.

"What ails ye?" asked his mother, looking at him curiously; "are ye not feeling well the morning, maybe now?"

"He's thinking along of Annie Maria Doyle," impudently explained younger brother Tim, ten years old.

"Tiger" reached over the hand of a champion and swept the small McQuirk from his chair.

"I feel fine," said he, "beyond a touch of the I-don't-know-what-you-call-its. I feel like there was going to be earthquakes or music or a trifle of chills and fever or maybe a picnic. I don't know how I feel. I feel like knocking the face off a policeman, or else maybe like playing Coney Island straight across the board from pop-corn to the elephant houdahs."

"It's the spring in yer bones," said Mrs. McQuirk. "It's the sap risin'. Time was when I couldn't keep me feet still nor me head cool when the earthworms began to crawl out in the dew of the mornin'. 'Tis a bit of tea will do ye good, made from pipsissewa and gentian bark at the druggist's."

"Back up!" said Mr. McQuirk, impatiently. "There's no spring in sight. There's snow yet on the shed in Donovan's backyard. And yesterday they puts open cars on the Sixth Avenue lines, and the janitors have quit ordering coal. And that means six weeks more of winter, by all the signs that be."

After breakfast Mr. McQuirk spent fifteen minutes before the corrugated mirror, subjugating his hair and arranging his green-and-purple ascot with its amethyst tombstone pin — eloquent of his chosen calling.

Since the strike had been called it was this particular striker's habit to hie himself each morning to the corner saloon of Flaherty Brothers, and there establish himself upon the sidewalk, with one foot resting on the bootblack's stand, observing the panorama of the street until the pace of time brought twelve o'clock and the dinner hour. And Mr. " Tiger " McQuirk, with his athletic seventy inches, well trained in sport and battle; his smooth, pale, solid, amiable face — blue where the razor had travelled; his carefully considered clothes and air of capability, was himself a spectacle not displeasing to the eye.

But on this morning Mr. McQuirk did not hasten immediately to his post of leisure and observation. Something unusual that he could not quite grasp was in the air. Something disturbed his thoughts, ruffled his senses, made him at once languid, irritable, elated, dissastisfied and sportive. He was no diagnostician, and he did not know that Lent was breaking up physiologically in his system.

Mrs. McQuirk had spoken of spring. Sceptically " Tiger " looked about him for signs. Few they were. The organ-grinders were at work; but they were always precocious harbingers. It was near enough spring for them to go penny-hunting when the skating ball dropped at the park. In the milliners' windows Easter hats, grave, gay and jubilant, blossomed. There were green patches among the sidewalk débris of the grocers. On a third-story windowsill the first elbow cushion of the season — old gold stripes on a crimson ground — supported the kimonoed arms of a pensive brunette. The wind blew cold from the East River, but the sparrows were flying to the eaves with straws. A second-hand store, combining foresight with faith, had set out an ice-chest and baseball goods.

And then " Tiger's " eye, discrediting these signs, fell upon one that bore a bud of promise. From a bright, new lithograph the head of Capricornus confronted him, betokening the forward and heady brew.

Mr. McQuirk entered the saloon and called for his glass of bock. He threw his nickel on the bar, raised the glass, set it down without tasting it and strolled toward the door.

"Wot's the matter, Lord Bolinbroke?" inquired the sarcastic bartender; "want a chiny vase or a gold-lined épergne to drink it out of — hey?"

"Say," said Mr. McQuirk, wheeling and shooting out a horizontal hand and a forty-five-degree chin, "you know your place only when it comes for givin' titles. I've changed me mind about drinkin'— see?

You got your money, ain't you? Wait till you get stung before you get the droop to your lip, will you?"

Thus Mr. Quirk added mutability of desires to the strange humors that had taken possession of him.

Leaving the saloon, he walked away twenty steps and leaned in the open doorway of Lutz, the barber. He and Lutz were friends, masking their sentiments behind abuse and bludgeons of repartee.

"Irish loafer," roared Lutz, "how do you do? So, not yet haf der bolicemans or der catcher of dogs done deir duty!"

"Hello, Dutch," said Mr. McQuirk. "Can't get your mind off of frankfurters, can you?"

"Bah!" exclaimed the German, coming and leaning in the door. "I haf a soul above frankfurters to-day. Dere is springtime in der air. I can feel it coming in ofer der mud of der streets and das ice in der river. Soon will dere be bicnics in der islands, mit kegs of beer under der trees."

"Say," said Mr. McQuirk, setting his hat on one side, "is everybody kiddin' me about gentle Spring? There ain't any more spring in the air than there is in a horsehair sofa in a Second Avenue furnished room. For me the winter underwear yet and the buckwheat cakes."

"You haf no boetry," said Lutz. "True, it is yedt cold, und in der city we haf not many of der signs; but dere are dree kinds of beoble dot should always feel der approach of spring first — dey are boets, lovers and poor vidows."

Mr. McQuirk went on his way, still possessed by the strange perturbation that he did not understand. Something was lacking to his comfort, and it made him half angry because he did not know what it was.

Two blocks away he came upon a foe, one Conover, whom he was bound in honor to engage in combat.

Mr. McQuirk made the attack with the characteristic suddenness and fierceness that had gained for him the endearing sobriquet of " Tiger." The defence of Mr. Conover was so prompt and admirable that the conflict was protracted until the onlookers unselfishly gave the warning cry of " Cheese it — the cop!" The principals escaped easily by running through the nearest open doors into the communicating backyards at the rear of the houses.

Mr. McQuirk emerged into another street. He stood by a lamp-post for a few minutes engaged in thought and then he turned and plunged into a small notion and news shop. A red-haired young woman, eating gum-drops, came and looked freezingly at him across the ice-bound steppes of the counter.

" Say, lady," he said, " have you got a song book with this in it. Let's see how it leads off —

" When the springtime comes we'll wander in the dale, love,
And whisper of those days of yore——"

" I'm having a friend," explained Mr. McQuirk,

" laid up with a broken leg, and he sent me after it. He's a devil for songs and poetry when he can't get out to drink."

" We have not," replied the young woman, with unconcealed contempt. " But there is a new song out that begins this way:

" ' Let us sit together in the old arm-chair;
And while the firelight flickers we'll be comfortable there.' "

There will be no profit in following Mr. " Tiger " McQuirk through his further vagaries of that day until he comes to stand knocking at the door of Annie Maria Doyle. The goddess Eastre, it seems, had guided his footsteps aright at last.

" Is that you now, Jimmy McQuirk? " she cried, smiling through the opened door (Annie Maria had never accepted the " Tiger "). " Well, whatever! "

" Come out in the hall," said Mr. McQuirk. " I want to ask yer opinion of the weather — on the level."

" Are you crazy, sure? " said Annie Maria.

" I am," said the " Tiger." " They've been telling me all day there was spring in the air. Were they liars? Or am I? "

" Dear me! " said Annie Maria —" haven't you noticed it? I can almost smell the violets. And the green grass. Of course, there ain't any yet — it's just a kind of feeling, you know."

" That's what I'm getting at," said Mr. McQuirk.

"I've had it. I didn't recognize it at first. I thought maybe it was en-wee, contracted the other day when I stepped above Fourteenth Street. But the katzenjammer I've got don't spell violets. It spells yer own name, Annie Maria, and it's you I want. I go to work next Monday, and I make four dollars a day. Spiel up, old girl — do we make a team?"

"Jimmy," sighed Annie Maria, suddenly disappearing in his overcoat, "don't you see that spring is all over the world right this minute?"

But you yourself remember how that day ended. Beginning with so fine a promise of vernal things, late in the afternoon the air chilled and an inch of snow fell — even so late in March. On Fifth Avenue the ladies drew their winter furs close about them. Only in the florists' windows could be perceived any signs of the morning smile of the coming goddess Eastre.

At six o'clock Herr Lutz began to close his shop. He heard a well-known shout: "Hello, Dutch!"

"Tiger" McQuirk, in his shirt-sleeves, with his hat on the back of his head, stood outside in the whirling snow, puffing at a black cigar.

"Donnerwetter!" shouted Lutz, "der vinter, he has gome back again yet!"

"Yer a liar, Dutch," called back Mr. McQuirk, with friendly geniality, "it's springtime, by the watch."

THE FOOL-KILLER

DOWN South whenever any one perpetrates some particularly monumental piece of foolishness everybody says: "Send for Jesse Holmes."

Jesse Holmes is the Fool-Killer. Of course he is a myth, like Santa Claus and Jack Frost and General Prosperity and all those concrete conceptions that are supposed to represent an idea that Nature has failed to embody. The wisest of the Southrons cannot tell you whence comes the Fool-Killer's name; but few and happy are the households from the Roanoke to the Rio Grande in which the name of Jesse Holmes has not been pronounced or invoked. Always with a smile, and often with a tear, is he summoned to his official duty. A busy man is Jesse Holmes.

I remember the clear picture of him that hung on the walls of my fancy during my barefoot days when I was dodging his oft-threatened devoirs. To me he was a terrible old man, in gray clothes, with a long, ragged, gray beard, and reddish, fierce eyes. I looked to see him come stumping up the road in a cloud of dust, with a white oak staff in his hand and his shoes tied with leather thongs. I may yet ——

157

But this is a story, not a sequel.

I have taken notice with regret, that few stories worth reading have been written that did not contain drink of some sort. Down go the fluids, from Arizona Dick's three fingers of red pizen to the inefficacious Oolong that nerves Lionel Montressor to repartee in the " Dotty Dialogues." So, in such good company I may introduce an absinthe drip — one absinthe drip, dripped through a silver dripper, orderly, opalescent, cool, green-eyed — deceptive.

Kerner was a fool. Besides that, he was an artist and my good friend. Now, if there is one thing on earth utterly despicable to another, it is an artist in the eyes of an author whose story he has illustrated. Just try it once. Write a story about a mining camp in Idaho. Sell it. Spend the money, and then, six months later, borrow a quarter (or a dime), and buy the magazine containing it. You find a full-page wash drawing of your hero, Black Bill, the cowboy. Somewhere in your story you employed the word " horse." Aha! the artist has grasped the idea. Black Bill has on the regulation trousers of the M. F. H. of the Westchester County Hunt. He carries a parlor rifle, and wears a monocle. In the distance is a section of Forty-second Street during a search for a lost gas-pipe, and the Taj Mahal, the famous mausoleum in India.

Enough! I hated Kerner, and one day I met him

and we became friends. He was young and gloriously melancholy because his spirits were so high and life had so much in store for him. Yes, he was almost riotously sad. That was his youth. When a man begins to be hilarious in a sorrowful way you can bet a million that he is dyeing his hair. Kerner's hair was plentiful and carefully matted as an artist's thatch should be. He was a cigaretteur, and he audited his dinners with red wine. But, most of all, he was a fool. And, wisely, I envied him, and listened patiently while he knocked Velasquez and Tintoretto. Once he told me that he liked a story of mine that he had come across in an anthology. He described it to me, and I was sorry that Mr. Fitz-James O'Brien was dead and could not learn of the eulogy of his work. But mostly Kerner made few breaks and was a consistent fool.

I'd better explain what I mean by that. There was a girl. Now, a girl, as far as I am concerned, is a thing that belongs in a seminary or an album; but I conceded the existence of the animal in order to retain Kerner's friendship. He showed me her picture in a locket — she was a blonde or a brunette — I have forgotten which. She worked in a factory for eight dollars a week. Lest factories quote this wage by way of vindication, I will add that the girl had worked for five years to reach that supreme elevation of remuneration, beginning at $1.50 per week.

Kerner's father was worth a couple of millions. He was willing to stand for art, but he drew the line at the factory girl. So Kerner disinherited his father and walked out to a cheap studio and lived on sausages for breakfast and on Farroni for dinner. Farroni had the artistic soul and a line of credit for painters and poets, nicely adjusted. Sometimes Kerner sold a picture and bought some new tapestry, a ring and a dozen silk cravats, and paid Farroni two dollars on account.

One evening Kerner had me to dinner with himself and the factory girl. They were to be married as soon as Kerner could slosh paint profitably. As for the ex-father's two millions — pouf!

She was a wonder. Small and half-way pretty, and as much at her ease in that cheap café as though she were only in the Palmer House, Chicago, with a souvenir spoon already safely hidden in her shirt waist. She was natural. Two things I noticed about her especially. Her belt buckle was exactly in the middle of her back, and she didn't tell us that a large man with a ruby stick-pin had followed her up all the way from Fourteenth Street. Was Kerner such a fool? I wondered. And then I thought of the quantity of striped cuffs and blue glass beads that $2,000,000 can buy for the heathen, and I said to myself that he was. And then Elise — certainly that was her name — told us, merrily, that the brown spot on her waist

was caused by her landlady knocking at the door
while she (the girl — confound the English language)
was heating an iron over the gas jet, and she hid the
iron under the bedclothes until the coast was clear,
and there was the piece of chewing gum stuck
to it when she began to iron the waist, and — well,
I wondered how in the world the chewing gum
came to be there — don't they ever stop chewing
it?

A while after that — don't be impatient, the absinthe drip is coming now — Kerner and I were dining
at Farroni's. A mandolin and a guitar were being
attacked; the room was full of smoke in nice, long
crinkly layers just like the artists draw the steam
from a plum pudding on Christmas posters, and a
lady in a blue silk and gasolined gauntlets was beginning to hum an air from the Catskills.

" Kerner," said I, " you are a fool."

" Of course," said Kerner, " I wouldn't let her go
on working. Not my wife. What's the use to wait?
She's willing. I sold that water color of the Pali-
sades yesterday. We could cook on a two-burner gas
stove. You know the ragouts I can throw together?
Yes, I think we will marry next week."

" Kerner," said I, " you are a fool."

" Have an absinthe drip? " said Kerner, grandly.
" To-night you are the guest of Art in paying quantities. I think we will get a flat with a bath."

" I never tried one — I mean an absinthe drip," said I.

The waiter brought it and poured the water slowly over the ice in the dripper.

" It looks exactly like the Mississippi River water in the big bend below Natchez," said I, fascinated, gazing at the be-muddled drip.

" There are such flats for eight dollars a week," said Kerner.

" You are a fool," said I, and began to sip the filtration. " What you need," I continued, " is the official attention of one Jesse Holmes."

Kerner, not being a Southerner, did not comprehend, so he sat, sentimental, figuring on his flat in his sordid, artistic way, while I gazed into the green eyes of the sophisticated Spirit of Wormwood.

Presently I noticed casually that a procession of bacchantes limned on the wall immediately below the ceiling had begun to move, traversing the room from right to left in a gay and spectacular pilgrimage. I did not confide my discovery to Kerner. The artistic temperament is too high-strung to view such deviations from the natural laws of the art of kalsomining. I sipped my absinthe drip and sawed wormwood.

One absinthe drip is not much — but I said again to Kerner, kindly :

" You are a fool." And then, in the vernacular : " Jesse Holmes for yours."

And then I looked around and saw the Fool-Killer, as he had always appeared to my imagination, sitting at a nearby table, and regarding us with his reddish, fatal, relentless eyes. He was Jesse Holmes from top to toe; he had the long, gray, ragged beard, the gray clothes of ancient cut, the executioner's look, and the dusty shoes of one who had been called from afar. His eyes were turned fixedly upon Kerner. I shuddered to think that I had invoked him from his assiduous southern duties. I thought of flying, and then I kept my seat, reflecting that many men had escaped his ministrations when it seemed that nothing short of an appointment as Ambassador to Spain could save them from him. I had called my brother Kerner a fool and was in danger of hell fire. That was nothing; but I would try to save him from Jesse Holmes.

The Fool-Killer got up from his table and came over to ours. He rested his hands upon it, and turned his burning, vindictive eyes upon Kerner, ignoring me.

"You are a hopeless fool," he said to the artist. "Haven't you had enough of starvation yet? I offer you one more opportunity. Give up this girl and come back to your home. Refuse, and you must take the consequences."

The Fool-Killer's threatening face was within a foot of his victim's; but to my horror, Kerner made not the slightest sign of being aware of his presence.

"We will be married next week," he muttered absent-mindedly. "With my studio furniture and some second-hand stuff we can make out."

"You have decided your own fate," said the Fool-Killer, in a low but terrible voice. "You may consider yourself as one dead. You have had your last chance."

"In the moonlight," went on Kerner, softly, "we will sit under the skylight with our guitar and sing away the false delights of pride and money."

"On your own head be it," hissed the Fool-Killer, and my scalp prickled when I perceived that neither Kerner's eyes nor his ears took the slightest cognizance of Jesse Holmes. And then I knew that for some reason the veil had been lifted for me alone, and that I had been elected to save my friend from destruction at the Fool-Killer's hands. Something of the fear and wonder of it must have showed itself in my face.

"Excuse me," said Kerner, with his wan, amiable smile; "was I talking to myself? I think it is getting to be a habit with me."

The Fool-Killer turned and walked out of Farroni's.

"Wait here for me," said I, rising; "I must speak to that man. Had you no answer for him? Because you are a fool must you die like a mouse under his foot? Could you not utter one squeak in your own defence?"

"You are drunk," said Kerner, heartlessly. "No one addressed me."

"The destroyer of your mind," said I, "stood above you just now and marked you for his victim. You are not blind or deaf."

"I recognized no such person," said Kerner. "I have seen no one but you at this table. Sit down. Hereafter you shall have no more absinthe drips."

"Wait here," said I, furious; "if you don't care for your own life, I will save it for you."

I hurried out and overtook the man in gray half-way down the block. He looked as I had seen him in my fancy a thousand times — truculent, gray and awful. He walked with the white oak staff, and but for the street-sprinkler the dust would have been flying under his tread.

I caught him by the sleeve and steered him to a dark angle of a building. I knew he was a myth, and I did not want a cop to see me conversing with vacancy, for I might land in Bellevue minus my silver matchbox and diamond ring.

"Jesse Holmes," said I, facing him with apparent bravery, "I know you. I have heard of you all my life. I know now what a scourge you have been to your country. Instead of killing fools you have been murdering the youth and genius that are necessary to

make a people live and grow great. You are a fool
yourself, Holmes; you began killing off the brightest
and best of your countrymen three generations ago,
when the old and obsolete standards of society and
honor and orthodoxy were narrow and bigoted. You
proved that when you put your murderous mark upon
my friend Kerner — the wisest chap I ever knew in
my life."

The Fool-Killer looked at me grimly and closely.

"You've a queer jag," said he, curiously. "Oh,
yes; I see who you are now. You were sitting with
him at the table. Well, if I'm not mistaken, I heard
you call him a fool, too."

"I did," said I. "I delight in doing so. It is
from envy. By all the standards that you know he is
the most egregious and grandiloquent and gorgeous
fool in all the world. That's why you want to kill
him."

"Would you mind telling me who or what you think
I am?" asked the old man.

I laughed boisterously and then stopped suddenly,
for I remembered that it would not do to be seen so
hilarious in the company of nothing but a brick
wall.

"You are Jesse Holmes, the Fool-Killer," I said,
solemnly, "and you are going to kill my friend Kerner. I don't know who rang you up, but if you do
kill him I'll see that you get pinched for it. That

is," I added, despairingly, " if I can get a cop to see you. They have a poor eye for mortals, and I think it would take the whole force to round up a myth murderer."

" Well," said the Fool-Killer, briskly, " I must be going. You had better go home and sleep it off. Good-night."

At this I was moved by a sudden fear for Kerner to a softer and more pleading mood. I leaned against the gray man's sleeve and besought him:

" Good Mr. Fool-Killer, please don't kill little Kerner. Why can't you go back South and kill Congressmen and clay-eaters and let us alone? Why don't you go up on Fifth Avenue and kill millionaires that keep their money locked up and won't let young fools marry because one of 'em lives on the wrong street? Come and have a drink, Jesse. Will you never get on to your job? "

" Do you know this girl that your friend has made himself a fool about? " asked the Fool-Killer.

" I have the honor," said I, " and that's why I called Kerner a fool. He is a fool because he has waited so long before marrying her. He is a fool because he has been waiting in the hopes of getting the consent of some absurd two-million-dollar-fool parent or something of the sort."

" Maybe," said the Fool-Killer — " maybe I — I might have looked at it differently. Would you mind going back to the restaurant and bringing your friend Kerner here? "

" Oh, what's the use, Jesse," I yawned.   " He can't see you.   He didn't know you were talking to him at the table.   You are a fictitious character, you know."

" Maybe he can this time.   Will you go fetch him? "

" All right," said I, " but I've a suspicion that you're not strictly sober, Jesse.   You seem to be wavering and losing your outlines.   Don't vanish before I get back."

I went back to Kerner and said:

" There's a man with an invisible homicidal mania waiting to see you outside.   I believe he wants to murder you.   Come along.   You won't see him, so there's nothing to be frightened about."

Kerner looked anxious.

" Why," said he, " I had no idea one absinthe would do that.   You'd better stick to Würzburger. I'll walk home with you."

I led him to Jesse Holmes's.

" Rudolf," said the Fool-Killer, " I'll give in. Bring her up to the house.   Give me your hand, boy."

" Good for you, dad," said Kerner, shaking hands with the old man.   " You'll never regret it after you know her."

"So, you did see him when he was talking to you at the table?" I asked Kerner.

"We hadn't spoken to each other in a year," said Kerner. "It's all right now."

I walked away.

"Where are you going?" called Kerner.

"I am going to look for Jesse Holmes," I answered, with dignity and reserve.

TRANSIENTS IN ARCADIA

THERE is a hotel on Broadway that has escaped discovery by the summer-resort promoters. It is deep and wide and cool. Its rooms are finished in dark oak of a low temperature. Home-made breezes and deep-green shrubbery give it the delights without the inconveniences of the Adirondacks. One can mount its broad staircases or glide dreamily upward in its aërial elevators, attended by guides in brass buttons, with a serene joy that Alpine climbers have never attained. There is a chef in its kitchen who will prepare for you brook trout better than the White Mountains ever served, sea food that would turn Old Point Comfort — "by Gad, sah!" — green with envy, and Maine venison that would melt the official heart of a game warden.

A few have found out this oasis in the July desert of Manhattan. During that month you will see the hotel's reduced array of guests scattered luxuriously about in the cool twilight of its lofty dining-room, gazing at one another across the snowy waste of unoccupied tables, silently congratulatory.

Superfluous, watchful, pneumatically moving waiters hover near, supplying every want before it is expressed. The temperature is perpetual April. The ceiling is painted in water colors to counterfeit a summer sky across which delicate clouds drift and do not vanish as those of nature do to our regret.

The pleasing, distant roar of Broadway is transformed in the imagination of the happy guests to the noise of a waterfall filling the woods with its restful sound. At every strange footstep the guests turn an anxious ear, fearful lest their retreat be discovered and invaded by the restless pleasure-seekers who are forever hounding nature to her deepest lairs.

Thus in the depopulated caravansary the little band of connoisseurs jealously hide themselves during the heated season, enjoying to the uttermost the delights of mountain and seashore that art and skill have gathered and served to them.

In this July came to the hotel one whose card that she sent to the clerk for her name to be registered read " Mme. Héloise D'Arcy Beaumont."

Madame Beaumont was a guest such as the Hotel Lotus loved. She possessed the fine air of the élite, tempered and sweetened by a cordial graciousness that made the hotel employés her slaves. Bell-boys fought for the honor of answering her ring; the clerks, but for the question of ownership, would have deeded to her the hotel and its contents; the other guests regarded her as the final touch of feminine exclusiveness and beauty that rendered the entourage perfect.

This super-excellent guest rarely left the hotel. Her habits were consonant with the customs of the discriminating patrons of the Hotel Lotus. To enjoy that delectable hostelry one must forego the city as though it were leagues away. By night a brief excursion to the nearby roofs is in order; but during the torrid day one remains in the umbrageous fastnesses of the Lotus as a trout hangs poised in the pellucid sanctuaries of his favorite pool.

Though alone in the Hotel Lotus, Madame Beaumont preserved the state of a queen whose loneliness was of position only. She breakfasted at ten, a cool, sweet, leisurely, delicate being who glowed softly in the dimness like a jasmine flower in the dusk.

But at dinner was Madame's glory at its height. She wore a gown as beautiful and immaterial as the mist from an unseen cataract in a mountain gorge. The nomenclature of this gown is beyond the guess of the scribe. Always pale-red roses reposed against its lace-garnished front. It was a gown that the head-waiter viewed with respect and met at the door. You thought of Paris when you saw it, and maybe of mysterious countesses, and certainly of Versailles and rapiers and Mrs. Fiske and rouge-et-noir. There was an untraceable rumor in the Hotel Lotus that Madame was a cosmopolite, and that she was pulling with her slender white hands certain strings between the nations in the favor of Russia. Being a citi-

zeness of the world's smoothest roads it was small
wonder that she was quick to recognize in the refined
purlieus of the Hotel Lotus the most desirable spot in
America for a restful sojourn during the heat of mid-
summer.

On the third day of Madame Beaumont's residence
in the hotel a young man entered and registered himself as a guest. His clothing — to speak of his
points in approved order — was quietly in the mode;
his features good and regular; his expression that of
a poised and sophisticated man of the world. He informed the clerk that he would remain three or four
days, inquired concerning the sailing of European
steamships, and sank into the blissful inanition of the
nonpareil hotel with the contented air of a traveller in
his favorite inn.

The young man — not to question the veracity of
the register — was Harold Farrington. He drifted
into the exclusive and calm current of life in the Lotus
so tactfully and silently that not a ripple alarmed his
fellow-seekers after rest. He ate in the Lotus and
of its patronym, and was lulled into blissful peace
with the other fortunate mariners. In one day he
acquired his table and his waiter and the fear lest the
panting chasers after repose that kept Broadway
warm should pounce upon and destroy this contiguous
but covert haven.

After dinner on the next day after the arrival of

Harold Farrington Madame Beaumont dropped her handkerchief in passing out. Mr. Farrington recovered and returned it without the effusiveness of a seeker after acquaintance.

Perhaps there was a mystic freemasonry between the discriminating guests of the Lotus. Perhaps they were drawn one to another by the fact of their common good fortune in discovering the acme of summer resorts in a Broadway hotel. Words delicate in courtesy and tentative in departure from formality passed between the two. And, as if in the expedient atmosphere of a real summer resort, an acquaintance grew, flowered and fructified on the spot as does the mystic plant of the conjuror. For a few moments they stood on a balcony upon which the corridor ended, and tossed the feathery ball of conversation.

"One tires of the old resorts," said Madame Beaumont, with a faint but sweet smile. "What is the use to fly to the mountains or the seashore to escape noise and dust when the very people that make both follow us there?"

"Even on the ocean," remarked Farrington, sadly, "the Philistines be upon you. The most exclusive steamers are getting to be scarcely more than ferry boats. Heaven help us when the summer resorter discovers that the Lotus is further away from Broadway than Thousand Islands or Mackinac."

"I hope our secret will be safe for a week, any-

how," said Madame, with a sigh and a smile. "I do
not know where I would go if they should descend
upon the dear Lotus. I know of but one place so de-
lightful in summer, and that is the castle of Count
Polinski, in the Ural Mountains."

"I hear that Baden-Baden and Cannes are almost
deserted this season," said Farrington. "Year by
year the old resorts fall in disrepute. Perhaps many
others, like ourselves, are seeking out the quiet nooks
that are overlooked by the majority."

"I promise myself three days more of this delicious
rest," said Madame Beaumont. "On Monday the
Cedric sails."

Harold Farrington's eyes proclaimed his regret.
"I too must leave on Monday," he said, "but I do
not go abroad."

Madame Beaumont shrugged one round shoulder in
a foreign gesture.

"One cannot hide here forever, charming though it
may be. The château has been in preparation for me
longer than a month. Those house parties that one
must give — what a nuisance! But I shall never forget my week in the Hotel Lotus."

"Nor shall I," said Farrington in a low voice,
"and I shall never *forgive* the *Cedric*."

On Sunday evening, three days afterward, the two
sat at a little table on the same balcony. A discreet
waiter brought ices and small glasses of claret cup.

Madame Beaumont wore the same beautiful evening gown that she had worn each day at dinner. She seemed thoughtful. Near her hand on the table lay a small chatelaine purse. After she had eaten her ice she opened the purse and took out a one-dollar bill.

" Mr. Farrington," she said, with the smile that had won the Hotel Lotus, " I want to tell you something. I'm going to leave before breakfast in the morning, because I've got to go back to my work. I'm behind the hosiery counter at Casey's Mammoth Store, and my vacation's up at eight o'clock to-morrow. That paper dollar is the last cent I'll see till I draw my eight dollars salary next Saturday night. You're a real gentleman, and you've been good to me, and I wanted to tell you before I went.

" I've been saving up out of my wages for a year just for this vacation. I wanted to spend one week like a lady if I never do another one. I wanted to get up when I please instead of having to crawl out at seven every morning; and I wanted to live on the best and be waited on and ring bells for things just like rich folks do. Now I've done it, and I've had the happiest time I ever expect to have in my life. I'm going back to my work and my little hall bedroom satisfied for another year. I wanted to tell you about it, Mr. Farrington, because I — I thought you kind of liked me, and I — I liked you. But, oh, I couldn't help deceiving you up till now, for it was all just like a fairy tale to me. So I talked about Europe and the things I've read about in other countries, and made you think I was a great lady.

" This dress I've got on — it's the only one I have that's fit to wear — I bought from O'Dowd & Levinsky on the instalment plan.

" Seventy-five dollars is the price, and it was made to measure. I paid $10 down, and they're to collect $1 a week till it's paid for. That'll be about all I have to say, Mr. Farrington, except that my name is Mamie Siviter instead of Madame Beaumont, and I thank you for your attentions. This dollar will pay the instalment due on the dress to-morrow. I guess I'll go up to my room now."

Harold Farrington listened to the recital of the Lotus's loveliest guest with an impassive countenance. When she had concluded he drew a small book like a checkbook from his coat pocket. He wrote upon a blank form in this with a stub of pencil, tore out the leaf, tossed it over to his companion and took up the paper dollar.

" I've got to go to work, too, in the morning," he said, " and I might as well begin now. There's a receipt for the dollar instalment. I've been a collector for O'Dowd & Levinsky for three years. Funny, ain't it, that you and me both had the same idea about spending our vacation? I've always wanted to put up at a swell hotel, and I saved up out

of my twenty per, and did it. Say, Mame, how about
a trip to Coney Saturday night on the boat —
what?"

The face of the pseudo Madame Héloise D'Arcy
Beaumont beamed.

"Oh, you bet I'll go, Mr. Farrington. The store
closes at twelve on Saturdays. I guess Coney'll be
all right even if we did spend a week with the swells."

Below the balcony the sweltering city growled and
buzzed in the July night. Inside the Hotel Lotus
the tempered, cool shadows reigned, and the solicitous
waiter single-footed near the low windows, ready at
a nod to serve Madame and her escort.

At the door of the elevator Farrington took his
leave, and Madame Beaumont made her last ascent.
But before they reached the noiseless cage he said:
"Just forget that 'Harold Farrington,' will you?
— McManus is the name — James McManus. Some
call me Jimmy."

"Good-night, Jimmy," said Madame.

THE RATHSKELLER AND THE ROSE

MISS POSIE CARRINGTON had earned her success. She began life handicapped by the family name of "Boggs," in the small town known as Cranberry Corners. At the age of eighteen she had acquired the name of "Carrington" and a position in the chorus of a metropolitan burlesque company. Thence upward she had ascended by the legitimate and delectable steps of "broiler," member of the famous "Dickey-bird" octette, in the successful musical comedy, "Fudge and Fellows," leader of the potato-bug dance in "Fol-de-Rol," and at length to the part of the maid "'Toinette" in "The King's Bath-Robe," which captured the critics and gave her her chance. And when we come to consider Miss Carrington she is in the heydey of flattery, fame and fizz; and that astute manager, Herr Timothy Goldstein, has her signature to iron-clad papers that she will star the coming season in Dyde Rich's new play, "Paresis by Gaslight."

Promptly there came to Herr Timothy a capable twentieth-century young character actor by the name of Highsmith, who besought engagement as "Sol

179

Haytosser," the comic and chief male character part in " Paresis by Gaslight."

" My boy," said Goldstein, " take the part if you can get it. Miss Carrington won't listen to any of my suggestions. She has turned down half a dozen of the best imitators of the rural dub in the city. She declares she won't set a foot on the stage unless ' Haytosser ' is the best that can be raked up. She was raised in a village, you know, and when a Broadway orchid sticks a straw in his hair and tries to call himself a clover blossom she's on, all right. I asked her, in a sarcastic vein, if she thought Denman Thompson would make any kind of a show in the part. ' Oh, no,' says she. ' I don't want him or John Drew or Jim Corbett or any of these swell actors that don't know a turnip from a turnstile. I want the real article.' So, my boy, if you want to play ' Sol Haytosser ' you will have to convince Miss Carrington. Luck be with you."

Highsmith took the train the next day for Cranberry Corners. He remained in that forsaken and inanimate village three days. He found the Boggs family and corkscrewed their history unto the third and fourth generation. He amassed the facts and the local color of Cranberry Corners. The village had not grown as rapidly as had Miss Carrington. The actor estimated that it had suffered as few actual changes since the departure of its solitary follower

of Thespis as had a stage upon which " four years
is supposed to have elapsed." He absorbed Cranberry Corners and returned to the city of chameleon
changes.

It was in the rathskeller that Highsmith made the
hit of his histrionic career. There is no need to
name the place; there is but one rathskeller where
you could hope to find Miss Posie Carrington after a
performance of " The King's Bath-Robe."

There was a jolly small party at one of the tables
that drew many eyes. Miss Carrington, petite, marvellous, bubbling, electric, fame-drunken, shall be
named first. Herr Goldstein follows, sonorous, curly-
haired, heavy, a trifle anxious, as some bear that had
caught, somehow, a butterfly in his claws. Next,
a man condemned to a newspaper, sad, courted,
armed, analyzing for press agent's dross every sentence that was poured over him, eating his à la New-
burg in the silence of greatness. To conclude, a
youth with parted hair, a name that is ochre to red
journals and gold on the back of a supper check.
These sat at a table while the musicians played, while
waiters moved in the mazy performance of their duties
with their backs toward all who desired their service,
and all was bizarre and merry because it was nine feet
below the level of the sidewalk.

At 11.45 a being entered the rathskeller. The
first violin perceptibly flatted a C that should have

been natural; the clarionet blew a bubble instead of a grace note; Miss Carrington giggled and the youth with parted hair swallowed an olive seed.

Exquisitely and irreproachably rural was the new entry. A lank, disconcerted, hesitating young man it was, flaxen-haired, gaping of mouth, awkward, stricken to misery by the lights and company. His clothing was butternut, with bright blue tie, showing four inches of bony wrist and white-socked ankle. He upset a chair, sat in another one, curled a foot around a table leg and cringed at the approach of a waiter.

"You may fetch me a glass of lager beer," he said, in response to the discreet questioning of the servitor.

The eyes of the rathskeller were upon him. He was as fresh as a collard and as ingenuous as a hay rake. He let his eye rove about the place as one who regards, big-eyed, hogs in the potato patch. His gaze rested at length upon Miss Carrington. He rose and went to her table with a lateral, shining smile and a blush of pleased trepidation.

"How're ye, Miss Posie?" he said in accents not to be doubted. "Don't ye remember me — Bill Summers — the Summerses that lived back of the blacksmith shop? I reckon I've growed up some since ye left Cranberry Corners.

"'Liza Perry 'lowed I might see ye in the city

while I was here. You know 'Liza married Benny Stanfield, and she says —— "

" Ah, say ! " interrupted Miss Carrington, brightly, " Lize Perry is never married — what ! Oh, the freckles of her ! "

" Married in June," grinned the gossip, " and livin' in the old Tatum Place. Ham Riley perfessed religion ; old Mrs. Blithers sold her place to Cap'n Spooner ; the youngest Waters girl run away with a music teacher ; the court-house burned up last March ; your uncle Wiley was elected constable ; Matilda Hoskins died from runnin' a needle in her hand, and Tom Beedle is courtin' Sallie Lathrop — they say he don't miss a night but what he's settin' on their porch."

" The wall-eyed thing ! " exclaimed Miss Carrington, with asperity. " Why, Tom Beedle once — say, you folks, excuse me a while — this is an old friend of mine — Mr.— what was it ? Yes, Mr. Summers — Mr. Goldstein, Mr. Ricketts, Mr.—— Oh, what's yours ? ' Johnny ' 'll do — come on over here and tell me some more."

She swept him to an isolated table in a corner. Herr Goldstein shrugged his fat shoulders and beckoned to the waiter. The newspaper man brightened a little and mentioned absinthe. The youth with parted hair was plunged into melancholy. The guests of the rathskeller laughed, clinked glasses and enjoyed the comedy that Posie Carrington was treating them to after her regular performance. 'A few cynical ones whispered "press agent" and smiled wisely.

Posie Carrington laid her dimpled and desirable chin upon her hands, and forgot her audience — a faculty that had won her laurels for her.

"I don't seem to recollect any Bill Summers," she said, thoughtfully gazing straight into the innocent blue eyes of the rustic young man. "But I know the Summerses, all right. I guess there ain't many changes in the old town. You see any of my folks lately?"

And then Highsmith played his trump. The part of "Sol Haytosser" called for pathos as well as comedy. Miss Carrington should see that he could do that as well.

"Miss Posie," said "Bill Summers," "I was up to your folkeses house jist two or three days ago. No, there ain't many changes to speak of. The lilac bush by the kitchen window is over a foot higher, and the elm in the front yard died and had to be cut down. 'And yet it don't seem the same place that it used to be."

"How's ma?" asked Miss Carrington.

"She was settin' by the front door, crocheting a lamp-mat when I saw her last," said "Bill." "She's older'n she was, Miss Posie. But everything in the house looked jest the same. Your ma asked me to set

down. 'Don't touch that willow rocker, William,'
says she. ' It ain't been moved since Posie left; and
that's the apron she was hemmin', layin' over the arm
of it, jist as she flung it. I'm in hopes,' she goes on,
' that Posie'll finish runnin' out that hem some day.' "

Miss Carrington beckoned peremptorily to a
waiter.

"A pint of extra dry," she ordered, briefly; " and
give the check to Goldstein."

" The sun was shinin' in the door," went on the
chronicler from Cranberry, " and your ma was settin'
right in it. I asked her if she hadn't better move
back a little. ' William,' says she, ' when I get sot
down and lookin' down the road, I can't bear to move.
Never a day,' says she, ' but what I set here every
minute that I can spare and watch over them palin's
for Posie. She went away down that road in the
night, for we seen her little shoe tracks in the dust,
and somethin' tells me she'll come back that way ag'in
when she's weary of the world and begins to think
about her old mother.'

" When I was comin' away," concluded " Bill,"
" I pulled this off'n the bush by the front steps. I
thought maybe I might see you in the city, and I
knowed you'd like somethin' from the old home."

He took from his coat pocket a rose — a drooping,
yellow, velvet, odorous rose, that hung its head in
the foul atmosphere of that tainted rathskeller like

a virgin bowing before the hot breath of the lions in a Roman arena.

Miss Carrington's penetrating but musical laugh rose above the orchestra's rendering of " Bluebells."

" Oh, say ! " she cried, with glee, " ain't those poky places the limit? I just know that two hours at Cranberry Corners would give me the horrors now. Well, I'm awful glad to have seen you, Mr. Summers. I guess I'll hustle around to the hotel now and get my beauty sleep."

She thrust the yellow rose into the bosom of her wonderful, dainty, silken garments, stood up and nodded imperiously at Herr Goldstein.

Her three companions and " Bill Summers " attended her to her cab. When her flounces and streamers were all safely tucked inside she dazzled them with au revoirs from her shining eyes and teeth.

" Come around to the hotel and see me, Bill, before you leave the city," she called as the glittering cab rolled away.

Highsmith, still in his make-up, went with Herr Goldstein to a café booth.

" Bright idea, eh? " asked the smiling actor. " Ought to land ' Sol Haytosser ' for me, don't you think? The little lady never once tumbled."

" I didn't hear your conversation," said Goldstein, " but your make-up and acting was O. K. Here's to your success. You'd better call on Miss Carrington

early to-morrow and strike her for the part. I don't
see how she can keep from being satisfied with your
exhibition of ability."

At 11.45 A. M. on the next day Highsmith, handsome, dressed in the latest mode, confident, with a
fuchsia in his button-hole, sent up his card to Miss
Carrington in her select apartment hotel.

He was shown up and received by the actress's
French maid.

" I am sorree," said Mlle. Hortense, " but I am to
say this to all. It is with great regret. Mees Carrington have cancelled all engagements on the stage
and have returned to live in that — how you call that
town? Cranberry Cornaire! "

THE CLARION CALL

HALF of this story can be found in the records of the Police Department; the other half belongs behind the business counter of a newspaper office.

One afternoon two weeks after Millionaire Norcross was found in his apartment murdered by a burglar, the murderer, while strolling serenely down Broadway, ran plump against Detective Barney Woods.

"Is that you, Johnny Kernan?" asked Woods, who had been near-sighted in public for five years.

"No less," cried Kernan, heartily. "If it isn't Barney Woods, late and early of old Saint Jo! You'll have to show me! What are you doing East? Do the green-goods circulars get out that far?"

"I've been in New York some years," said Woods. "I'm on the city detective force."

"Well, well!" said Kernan, breathing smiling joy and patting the detective's arm.

"Come into Muller's," said Woods, "and let's hunt a quiet table. I'd like to talk to you awhile."

It lacked a few minutes to the hour of four. The tides of trade were not yet loosed, and they found a quiet corner of the café. Kernan, well dressed, slightly swaggering, self-confident, seated himself opposite the little detective, with his pale, sandy mustache, squinting eyes and ready-made cheviot suit.

"What business are you in now?" asked Woods.
"You know you left Saint Jo a year before I did."

"I'm selling shares in a copper mine," said Kernan. "I may establish an office here. Well, well! and so old Barney is a New York detective. You always had a turn that way. You were on the police in Saint Jo after I left there, weren't you?"

"Six months," said Woods. "And now there's one more question, Johnny. I've followed your record pretty close ever since you did that hotel job in Saratoga, and I never knew you to use your gun before. Why did you kill Norcross?"

Kernan stared for a few moments with concentrated attention at the slice of lemon in his high-ball; and then he looked at the detective with a sudden, crooked, brilliant smile.

"How did you guess it, Barney?" he asked, admiringly. "I swear I thought the job was as clean and as smooth as a peeled onion. Did I leave a string hanging out anywhere?"

Woods laid upon the table a small gold pencil intended for a watch-charm.

"It's the one I gave you the last Christmas we were in Saint Jo. I've got your shaving mug yet. I found this under a corner of the rug in Norcross's

room. I warn you to be careful what you say. I've
got it put on to you, Johnny. We were old friends
once, but I must do my duty. You'll have to go to
the chair for Norcross."

Kernan laughed.

"My luck stays with me," said he. "Who'd have
thought old Barney was on my trail!" He slipped
one hand inside his coat. In an instant Woods had
a revolver against his side.

"Put it away," said Kernan, wrinkling his nose.
"I'm only investigating. Aha! It takes nine tailors
to make a man, but one can do a man up. There's
a hole in that vest pocket. I took that pencil off my
chain and slipped it in there in case of a scrap. Put
up your gun, Barney, and I'll tell you why I had
to shoot Norcross. The old fool started down the
hall after me, popping at the buttons on the back of
my coat with a peevish little .22 and I had to stop
him. The old lady was a darling. She just lay in
bed and saw her $12,000 diamond necklace go with-
out a chirp, while she begged like a panhandler to
have back a little thin gold ring with a garnet worth
about $3. I guess she married old Norcross for his
money, all right. Don't they hang on to the little
trinkets from the Man Who Lost Out, though?
There were six rings, two brooches and a chatelaine
watch. Fifteen thousand would cover the lot."

"I warned you not to talk," said Woods.

" Oh, that's all right," said Kernan. " The stuff is in my suit case at the hotel. And now I'll tell you why I'm talking. Because it's safe. I'm talking to a man I know. You owe me a thousand dollars, Barney Woods, and even if you wanted to arrest me your hand wouldn't make the move."

" I haven't forgotten," said Woods. " You counted out twenty fifties without a word. I'll pay it back some day. That thousand saved me and — well, they were piling my furniture out on the sidewalk when I got back to the house."

" And so," continued Kernan, " you being Barney Woods, born as true as steel, and bound to play a white man's game, can't lift a finger to arrest the man you're indebted to. Oh, I have to study men as well as Yale locks and window fastenings in my business. Now, keep quiet while I ring for the waiter. I've had a thirst for a year or two that worries me a little. If I'm ever caught the lucky sleuth will have to divide honors with old boy Booze. But I never drink during business hours. After a job I can crook elbows with my old friend Barney with a clear conscience. What are you taking? "

The waiter came with the little decanters and the siphon and left them alone again.

" You've called the turn," said Woods, as he rolled the little gold pencil about with a thoughtful forefinger. " I've got to pass you up. I can't lay a hand on you. If I'd a-paid that money back — but I didn't, and that settles it. It's a bad break I'm making, Johnny, but I can't dodge it. You helped me once, and it calls for the same."

"I knew it," said Kernan, raising his glass, with a flushed smile of self-appreciation. "I can judge men. Here's to Barney, for —'he's a jolly good fellow.'"

"I don't believe," went on Woods quietly, as if he were thinking aloud, "that if accounts had been square between you and me, all the money in all the banks in New York could have bought you out of my hands to-night."

"I know it couldn't," said Kernan. "That's why I knew I was safe with you."

"Most people," continued the detective, "look side-ways at my business. They don't class it among the fine arts and the professions. But I've always taken a kind of fool pride in it. And here is where I go 'busted.' I guess I'm a man first and a detective afterward. I've got to let you go, and then I've got to resign from the force. I guess I can drive an express wagon. Your thousand dollars is further off than ever, Johnny."

"Oh, you're welcome to it," said Kernan, with a lordly air. "I'd be willing to call the debt off, but I know you wouldn't have it. It was a lucky day for me when you borrowed it. And now, let's drop the subject. I'm off to the West on a morning train. I know a place out there where I can negotiate the Norcross sparks. Drink up, Barney, and forget your troubles. We'll have a jolly time while the police are knocking their heads together over the case. I've got one of my Sahara thirsts on to-night. But I'm in the hands — the unofficial hands — of my old friend Barney, and I won't even dream of a cop."

And then, as Kernan's ready finger kept the button and the waiter working, his weak point — a tremendous vanity and arrogant egotism, began to show itself. He recounted story after story of his successful plunderings, ingenious plots and infamous transgressions until Woods, with all his familiarity with evil-doers, felt growing within him a cold abhorrence toward the utterly vicious man who had once been his benefactor.

"I'm disposed of, of course," said Woods, at length. "But I advise you to keep under cover for a spell. The newspapers may take up this Norcross affair. There has been an epidemic of burglaries and manslaughter in town this summer."

The word sent Kernan into a high glow of sullen and vindictive rage.

"To h—l with the newspapers," he growled. "What do they spell but brag and blow and boodle in box-car letters? Suppose they do take up a case — what does it amount to? The police are easy enough to fool; but what do the newspapers do? They send a lot of pin-head reporters around to the scene; and they make for the nearest saloon and have beer while they take photos of the bartender's oldest daughter in evening dress, to print as the fiancée of the young man in the tenth story, who thought he heard a noise below on the night of the murder. That's about as near as the newspapers ever come to running down Mr. Burglar."

"Well, I don't know," said Woods, reflecting. "Some of the papers have done good work in that line. There's the *Morning Mars*, for instance. It warmed up two or three trails, and got the man after the police had let 'em get cold."

"I'll show you," said Kernan, rising, and expanding his chest. "I'll show you what I think of newspapers in general, and your *Morning Mars* in particular."

Three feet from their table was the telephone booth. Kernan went inside and sat at the instrument, leaving the door open. He found a number in the book, took down the receiver and made his demand upon Central. Woods sat still, looking at the sneering, cold, vigilant face waiting close to the transmitter, and listened to the words that came from the thin, truculent lips curved into a contemptuous smile.

"That the *Morning Mars?* . . . I want to speak to the managing editor . . . Why, tell

him it's some one who wants to talk to him about the
Norcross murder.

" You the editor? . . . All right. . . . I
am the man who killed old Norcross . . . Wait!
Hold the wire; I'm not the usual crank . . . Oh,
there isn't the slightest danger. I've just been discussing it with a detective friend of mine. I killed
the old man at 2:30 A. M. two weeks ago to-
morrow. . . . Have a drink with you? Now,
hadn't you better leave that kind of talk to your
funny man? Can't you tell whether a man's guying
you or whether you're being offered the biggest scoop
your dull dishrag of a paper ever had? . . .
Well, that's so; it's a bobtail scoop — but you can
hardly expect me to 'phone in my name and address.
. . . Why? Oh, because I heard you make a
specialty of solving mysterious crimes that stump the
police. . . . No, that's not all. I want to tell
you that your rotten, lying, penny sheet is of no more
use in tracking an intelligent murderer or highway-
man than a blind poodle would be. . . . What?
. . . Oh, no, this isn't a rival newspaper office;
you're getting it straight. I did the Norcross job,
and I've got the jewels in my suit case at — ' the
name of the hotel could not be learned ' — you recognize that phrase, don't you? I thought so. You've
used it often enough. Kind of rattles you, doesn't
it, to have the mysterious villain call up your great,

big, all-powerful organ of right and justice and good
government and tell you what a helpless old gas-bag
you are? . . . Cut that out; you're not that big
a fool — no, you don't think I'm a fraud. I can tell
it by your voice. . . . Now, listen, and I'll give
you a pointer that will prove it to you. Of course
you've had this murder case worked over by your staff
of bright young blockheads. Half of the second button on old Mrs. Norcross's nightgown is broken off.
I saw it when I took the garnet ring off her finger.
I thought it was a ruby. . . . Stop that! it
won't work."

Kernan turned to Woods with a diabolic smile.

"I've got him going. He believes me now. He
didn't quite cover the transmitter with his hand when
he told somebody to call up Central on another 'phone
and get our number. I'll give him just one more dig,
and then we'll make a ' get-away.'

"Hello! . . . Yes. I'm here yet. You
didn't think I'd run from such a little subsidized, turn-
coat rag of a newspaper, did you? . . . Have
me inside of forty-eight hours? Say, will you quit
being funny? Now, you let grown men alone and at-
tend to your business of hunting up divorce cases
and street-car accidents and printing the filth and
scandal that you make your living by. Good-by, old
boy — sorry I haven't time to call on you. I'd feel
perfectly safe in your sanctum asinorum. Tra-la!"

" He's as mad as a cat that's lost a mouse," said Kernan, hanging up the receiver and coming out. " And now, Barney, my boy, we'll go to a show and enjoy ourselves until a reasonable bedtime. Four hours' sleep for me, and then the west-bound."

The two dined in a Broadway restaurant. Kernan was pleased with himself. He spent money like a prince of fiction. And then a weird and gorgeous musical comedy engaged their attention. Afterward there was a late supper in a grillroom, with champagne, and Kernan at the height of his complacency.

Half-past three in the morning found them in a corner of an all-night café, Kernan still boasting in a vapid and rambling way, Woods thinking moodily over the end that had come to his usefulness as an upholder of the law.

But, as he pondered, his eye brightened with a speculative light.

" I wonder if it's possible," he said to himself, " I won-der if it's pos-si-ble!"

And then outside the café the comparative stillness of the early morning was punctured by faint, uncertain cries that seemed mere fireflies of sound, some growing louder, some fainter, waxing and waning amid the rumble of milk wagons and infrequent cars. Shrill cries they were when near — well-known cries that conveyed many meanings to the ears of those of

the slumbering millions of the great city who waked
to hear them.   Cries that bore upon their significant,
small volume the weight of a world's woe and laughter and delight and stress.   To some, cowering beneath the protection of a night's ephemeral cover,
they brought news of the hideous, bright day; to
others, wrapped in happy sleep, they announced a
morning that would dawn blacker than sable night.
To many of the rich they brought a besom to sweep
away what had been theirs while the stars shone; to
the poor they brought — another day.

All over the city the cries were starting up, keen
and sonorous, heralding the chances that the slip-
ping of one cogwheel in the machinery of time had
made; apportioning to the sleepers while they lay
at the mercy of fate, the vengeance, profit, grief,
reward and doom that the new figure in the calen-
dar had brought them.   Shrill and yet plaintive
were the cries, as if the young voices grieved that so
much evil and so little good was in their irresponsible
hands.   Thus echoed in the streets of the helpless
city the transmission of the latest decrees of the gods,
the cries of the newsboys — the Clarion Call of the
Press.

Woods flipped a dime to the waiter, and said:
"Get me a *Morning Mars*."

When the paper came he glanced at its first page,
and then tore a leaf out of his memorandum book

and began to write on it with the little gold pencil.

"What's the news?" yawned Kernan.

Woods flipped over to him the piece of writing:

"The New York *Morning Mars:*
 "Please pay to the order of John Kernan the one thousand dollars reward coming to me for his arrest and conviction.
                                        "BARNARD WOODS."

"I kind of thought they would do that," said Woods, "when you were jollying 'em so hard. Now, Johnny, you'll come to the police station with me."

EXTRADITED FROM BOHEMIA

FROM near the village of Harmony, at the foot of the Green Mountains, came Miss Medora Martin to New York with her color-box and easel.

Miss Medora resembled the rose which the autumnal frosts had spared the longest of all her sister blossoms. In Harmony, when she started alone to the wicked city to study art, they said she was a mad, reckless, headstrong girl. In New York, when she first took her seat at a West Side boarding-house table, the boarders asked: " Who is the nice-looking old maid? "

Medora took heart, a cheap hall bedroom and two art lessons a week from Professor Angelini, a retired barber who had studied his profession in a Harlem dancing academy. There was no one to set her right, for here in the big city they do it unto all of us. How many of us are badly shaved daily and taught the two-step imperfectly by ex-pupils of Bastien Le Page and Gérôme? The most pathetic sight in New York — except the manners of the rush-hour crowds — is the dreary march of the hopeless army of Mediocrity. Here Art is no benignant goddess, but a Circe who turns her wooers into mewing Toms and Tabbies who linger about the doorsteps of her abode, unmindful of the flying brickbats and boot-jacks of the critics. Some of us creep back to our native villages to the skim-milk of " I told you so "; but most of us prefer to remain in the cold courtyard of our mistress's temple, snatching the scraps that fall from her divine table d'hôte. But some of us grow weary at last of the fruitless service. And then there are two fates open to us. We can get a job driving a grocer's wagon, or we can get swallowed up in the Vortex of Bohemia. The latter sounds good; but the former really pans out better. For, when the grocer pays us off we can rent a dress suit and — the capitalized system of humor describes it best — Get Bohemia On the Run.

Miss Medora chose the Vortex and thereby furnishes us with our little story.

Professor Angelini praised her sketches excessively. Once when she had made a neat study of a horse-chestnut tree in the park he declared she would become a second Rosa Bonheur. Again — a great artist has his moods — he would say cruel and cutting things. For example, Medora had spent an afternoon patiently sketching the statue and the architecture at Columbus Circle. Tossing it aside with a sneer, the professor informed her that Giotto had once drawn a perfect circle with one sweep of his hand.

One day it rained, the weekly remittance from Harmony was overdue, Medora had a headache, the professor had tried to borrow two dollars from her, her art dealer had sent back all her water-colors unsold, and — Mr. Binkley asked her out to dinner.

Mr. Binkley was the gay boy of the boarding-house. He was forty-nine, and owned a fishstall in a downtown market. But after six o'clock he wore an evening suit and whooped things up connected with the beaux arts. The young men said he was an " Indian." He was supposed to be an accomplished habitué of the inner circles of Bohemia. It was no secret that he had once loaned $10 to a young man who had had a drawing printed in *Puck*. Often has one thus obtained his entrée into the charmed circle, while the other obtained both his entrée and roast.

The other boarders enviously regarded Medora as she left at Mr. Binkley's side at nine o'clock. She was as sweet as a cluster of dried autumn grasses in her pale blue — oh — er — that very thin stuff — in her pale blue Comstockized silk waist and box-pleated voile skirt, with a soft pink glow on her thin cheeks and the tiniest bit of rouge powder on her face, with her handkerchief and room key in her brown walrus, pebble-grain hand-bag.

And Mr. Binkley looked imposing and dashing with his red face and gray mustache, and his tight dress coat, that made the back of his neck roll up just like a successful novelist's.

They drove in a cab to the Café Terence, just off the most glittering part of Broadway, which, as every one knows, is one of the most popular and widely patronized, jealously exclusive Bohemian resorts in the city.

Down between the rows of little tables tripped Medora, of the Green Mountains, after her escort. Thrice in a lifetime may woman walk upon clouds — once when she trippeth to the altar, once when she first enters Bohemian halls, the last when she marches back across her first garden with the dead hen of her neighbor in her hand.

There was a table set, with three or four about it. A waiter buzzed around it like a bee, and silver and glass shone upon it. And, preliminary to the meal, as the prehistoric granite strata heralded the protozoa, the bread of Gaul, compounded after the formula of the recipe for the eternal hills, was there set forth to the hand and tooth of a long-suffering city, while the gods lay beside their nectar and home-made biscuits and smiled, and the dentists leaped for joy in their gold-leafy dens.

The eye of Binkley fixed a young man at his table with the Bohemian gleam, which is a compound of the look of the Basilisk, the shine of a bubble of Würzburger, the inspiration of genius and the pleading of a panhandler.

The young man sprang to his feet. " Hello, Bink,

old boy!" he shouted. "Don't tell me you were going to pass our table. Join us — unless you've another crowd on hand."

"Don't mind, old chap," said Binkley, of the fishstall. "You know how I like to butt up against the
fine arts. Mr. Vandyke — Mr. Madder — er —
Miss Martin, one of the elect also in art — er ——"

The introduction went around. There were also
Miss Elise and Miss 'Toinette. Perhaps they were
models, for they chattered of the St. Regis decora-
tions and Henry James — and they did it not badly.

Medora sat in transport. Music — wild, intoxi-
cating music made by troubadours direct from a rear
basement room in Elysium — set her thoughts to
dancing. Here was a world never before penetrated
by her warmest imagination or any of the lines controlled by Harriman. With the Green Mountains'
external calm upon her she sat, her soul flaming in
her with the fire of Andalusia. The tables were filled
with Bohemia. The room was full of the fragrance
of flowers — both mille and cauli. Questions and
corks popped; laughter and silver rang; champagne
flashed in the pail, wit flashed in the pan.

Vandyke ruffled his long, black locks, disarranged
his careless tie and leaned over to Madder.

"Say, Maddy," he whispered, feelingly, "sometimes I'm tempted to pay this Philistine his ten dollars and get rid of him."

Madder ruffled his long, sandy locks and disarranged his careless tie.

"Don't think of it, Vandy," he replied. "We are short, and Art is long."

Medora ate strange viands and drank elderberry wine that they poured in her glass. It was just the color of that in the Vermont home. The waiter poured something in another glass that seemed to be boiling, but when she tasted it it was not hot. She had never felt so light-hearted before. She thought lovingly of the Green Mountain farm and its fauna. She leaned, smiling, to Miss Elise.

"If I were at home," she said, beamingly, "I could show you the cutest little calf!"

"Nothing for you in the White Lane," said Miss Elise. "Why don't you pad?"

The orchestra played a wailing waltz that Medora had learned from the hand-organs. She followed the air with nodding head in a sweet soprano hum. Madder looked across the table at her, and wondered in what strange waters Binkley had caught her in his seine. She smiled at him, and they raised glasses and drank of the wine that boiled when it was cold. Binkley had abandoned art and was prating of the unusual spring catch of shad. Miss Elise arranged the palette-and-maul-stick tie pin of Mr. Vandyke. A Philistine at some distant table was maundering volubly either about Jerome or Gérôme. A famous actress was discoursing excitably about monogrammed hosiery. A hose clerk from a department store was loudly proclaiming his opinions of the drama. A writer was abusing Dickens. A magazine editor and a photographer were drinking a dry brand at a reserved table. A 36-25-42 young lady was saying to an eminent sculptor: " Fudge for your Prax Italys! Bring one of your Venus Anno Dominis down to Cohen's and see how quick she'd be turned down for a cloak model. Back to the quarries with your Greeks and Dagos! "

Thus went Bohemia.

At eleven Mr. Binkley took Medora to the boarding-house and left her, with a society bow, at the foot of the hall stairs. She went up to her room and lit the gas.

And then, as suddenly as the dreadful genie arose in vapor from the copper vase of the fisherman, arose in that room the formidable shape of the New England Conscience. The terrible thing that Medora had done was revealed to her in its full enormity. She had sat in the presence of the ungodly and looked upon the wine both when it was red and effervescent.

At midnight she wrote this letter:

" Mr. BERIAH HOSKINS, Harmony, Vermont.

" Dear Sir: Henceforth, consider me as dead to

you forever. I have loved you too well to blight your career by bringing into it my guilty and sin-stained life. I have succumbed to the insidious wiles of this wicked world and have been drawn into the vortex of Bohemia. There is scarcely any depth of glittering iniquity that I have not sounded. It is hopeless to combat my decision. There is no rising from the depths to which I have sunk. Endeavor to forget me. I am lost forever in the fair but brutal maze of awful Bohemia. Farewell.

" ONCE YOUR MEDORA."

On the next day Medora formed her resolutions. Beelzebub, flung from heaven, was no more cast down. Between her and the apple blossoms of Harmony there was a fixed gulf. Flaming cherubim warded her from the gates of her lost paradise. In one evening, by the aid of Binkley and Mumm, Bohemia had gathered her into its awful midst.

There remained to her but one thing — a life of brilliant, but irremediable error. Vermont was a shrine that she never would dare to approach again. But she would not sink — there were great and compelling ones in history upon whom she would model her meteoric career — Camille, Lola Montez, Royal Mary, Zaza — such a name as one of these would that of Medora Martin be to future generations.

For two days Medora kept her room. On the

third she opened a magazine at the portrait of the
King of Belgium, and laughed sardonically. If that
far-famed breaker of women's hearts should cross her
path, he would have to bow before her cold and im-
perious beauty. She would not spare the old or
the young. All America — all Europe should do
homage to her sinister, but compelling charm.

As yet she could not bear to think of the life she
had once desired — a peaceful one in the shadow of
the Green Mountains with Beriah at her side, and
orders for expensive oil paintings coming in by each
mail from New York. Her one fatal misstep had
shattered that dream.

On the fourth day Medora powdered her face and
rouged her lips. Once she had seen Carter in
" Zaza." She stood before the mirror in a reckless
attitude and cried: " *Zut! zut!* " She rhymed it
with " nut," but with the lawless word Harmony
seemed to pass away forever. The Vortex had her.
She belonged to Bohemia for evermore. And never
would Beriah ——

The door opened and Beriah walked in.

" 'Dory," said he, " what's all that chalk and pink
stuff on your face, honey? "

Medora extended an arm.

" Too late," she said, solemnly. " The die is cast.
I belong in another world. Curse me if you will —
it is your right. Go, and leave me in the path I

have chosen. Bid them all at home never to mention my name again. And sometimes, Beriah, pray for me when I am revelling in the gaudy, but hollow, pleasures of Bohemia."

"Get a towel, 'Dory," said Beriah, "and wipe that paint off your face. I came as soon as I got your letter. Them pictures of yours ain't amounting to anything. I've got tickets for both of us back on the evening train. Hurry and get your things in your trunk."

"Fate was too strong for me, Beriah. Go while I am strong to bear it."

"How do you fold this easel, 'Dory? — now begin to pack, so we have time to eat before train time. The maples is all out in full-grown leaves, 'Dory — you just ought to see 'em!"

"Not this early, Beriah?"

"You ought to see 'em, 'Dory; they're like an ocean of green in the morning sunlight."

"Oh, Beriah!"

On the train she said to him suddenly:

"I wonder why you came when you got my letter."

"Oh, shucks!" said Beriah. "Did you think you could fool me? How could you be run away to that Bohemia country like you said when your letter was postmarked New York as plain as day?"

A PHILISTINE IN BOHEMIA

GEORGE WASHINGTON, with his right arm up-raised, sits his iron horse at the lower corner of Union Square, forever signalling the Broadway cars to stop as they round the curve into Fourteenth Street. But the cars buzz on, heedless, as they do at the beck of a private citizen, and the great General must feel, unless his nerves are iron, that rapid transit gloria mundi.

Should the General raise his left hand as he has raised his right it would point to a quarter of the city that forms a haven for the oppressed and suppressed of foreign lands. In the cause of national or personal freedom they have found a refuge here, and the patriot who made it for them sits his steed, overlooking their district, while he listens through his left ear to vaudeville that caricatures the posterity of his protégés. Italy, Poland, the former Spanish possessions and the polyglot tribes of Austria-Hungary have spilled here a thick lather of their effervescent sons. In the eccentric cafés and lodging-houses of the vicinity they hover over their native wines and political secrets. The colony changes with much frequency. Faces disappear from the

haunts to be replaced by others. Whither do these
uneasy birds flit? For half of the answer observe
carefully the suave foreign air and foreign courtesy
of the next waiter who serves your table d'hôte.
For the other half, perhaps if the barber shops had
tongues (and who will dispute it?) they could tell
their share.

Titles are as plentiful as finger rings among these
transitory exiles. For lack of proper exploitation a
stock of titled goods large enough to supply the trade
of upper Fifth Avenue is here condemned to a mere
pushcart traffic. The new-world landlords who en-
tertain these offshoots of nobility are not dazzled
by coronets and crests. They have doughnuts to
sell instead of daughters. With them it is a serious
matter of trading in flour and sugar instead of pearl
powder and bonbons.

These assertions are deemed fitting as an introduction to the tale, which is of plebeians and contains
no one with even the ghost of a title.

Katy Dempsey's mother kept a furnished-room
house in this oasis of the aliens. The business was
not profitable. If the two scraped together enough
to meet the landlord's agent on rent day and negotiate for the ingredients of a daily Irish stew they
called it success. Often the stew lacked both meat
and potatoes. Sometimes it became as bad as con-
sommé with music.

In this mouldy old house Katy waxed plump and pert and wholesome and as beautiful and freckled as a tiger lily. She was the good fairy who was guilty of placing the damp clean towels and cracked pitchers of freshly laundered Croton in the lodgers' rooms.

You are informed (by virtue of the privileges of astronomical discovery) that the star lodger's name was Mr. Brunelli. His wearing a yellow tie and paying his rent promptly distinguished him from the other lodgers. His raiment was splendid, his complexion olive, his mustache fierce, his manners a prince's, his rings and pins as magnificent as those of a travelling dentist.

He had breakfast served in his room, and he ate it in a red dressing gown with green tassels. He left the house at noon and returned at midnight. Those were mysterious hours, but there was nothing mysterious about Mrs. Dempsey's lodgers except the things that were not mysterious. One of Mr. Kipling's poems is addressed to "Ye who hold the unwritten clue to all save all unwritten things." The same "readers" are invited to tackle the foregoing assertion.

Mr. Brunelli, being impressionable and a Latin, fell to conjugating the verb "amare," with Katy in the objective case, though not because of antipathy. She talked it over with her mother.

"Sure, I like him," said Katy. "He's more politeness than twinty candidates for Alderman, and he makes me feel like a queen whin he walks at me side. But what is he, I dinno? I've me suspicions. The marnin'll coom whin he'll throt out the picture av his baronial halls and ax to have the week's rint hung up in the ice chist along wid all the rist of 'em."

" 'Tis thrue," admitted Mrs. Dempsey, " that he seems to be a sort iv a Dago, and too coolchured in his spache for a rale gintleman. But ye may be mis-judgin' him. Ye should niver suspect any wan of bein' of noble descint that pays cash and pathronizes the laundry rig'lar."

" He's the same thricks of spakin' and blarneyin' wid his hands," sighed Katy, " as the Frinch noble-man at Mrs. Toole's that ran away wid Mr. Toole's Sunday pants and left the photograph of the Bastile, his grandfather's chat-taw, as security for tin weeks' rint."

Mr. Brunelli continued his calorific wooing. Katy continued to hesitate. One day he asked her out to dine and she felt that a dénouement was in the air. While they are on their way, with Katy in her best muslin, you must take as an entr'acte a brief peep at New York's Bohemia.

'Tonio's restaurant is in Bohemia. The very lo-cation of it is secret. If you wish to know where it is ask the first person you meet. He will tell you in a whisper. 'Tonio discountenances custom; he keeps

his house-front black and forbidding; he gives you a
pretty bad dinner; he locks his door at the dining
hour; but he knows spaghetti as the boarding-house
knows cold veal; and — he has deposited many dollars in a certain Banco di —— something with many
gold vowels in the name on its windows.

To this restaurant Mr. Brunelli conducted Katy.
The house was dark and the shades were lowered; but
Mr. Brunelli touched an electric button by the base-
ment door, and they were admitted.

Along a long, dark, narrow hallway they went and
then through a shining and spotless kitchen that
opened directly upon a back yard.

The walls of houses hemmed three sides of the
yard; a high, board fence, surrounded by cats, the
other. A wash of clothes was suspended high upon
a line stretched from diagonal corners. Those were
property clothes, and were never taken in by 'Tonio.
They were there that wits with defective pronuncia-
tion might make puns in connection with the ragout.

A dozen and a half little tables set upon the bare
ground were crowded with Bohemia-hunters, who
flocked there because 'Tonio pretended not to want
them and pretended to give them a good dinner.
There was a sprinkling of real Bohemians present
who came for a change because they were tired of
the real Bohemia, and a smart shower of the men
who originate the bright sayings of Congressmen and

the little nephew of the well-known general passenger agent of the Evansville and Terre Haute Railroad Company.

Here is a bon mot that was manufactured at 'Tonio's:

" A dinner at 'Tonio's," said a Bohemian, " always amounts to twice the price that is asked for it."

Let us assume that an accommodating voice inquires:

" How so? "

" The dinner costs you 40 cents; you give 10 cents to the waiter, and it makes you feel like 30 cents."

Most of the diners were confirmed table d'hôters — gastronomic adventuress, forever seeking the El Dorado of a good claret, and consistently coming to grief in California.

Mr. Brunelli escorted Katy to a little table embowered with shrubbery in tubs, and asked her to excuse him for a while.

Katy sat, enchanted by a scene so brilliant to her. The grand ladies, in splendid dresses and plumes and sparkling rings; the fine gentlemen who laughed so loudly, the cries of " Garsong! " and " We, monseer," and " Hello, Mame! " that distinguish Bohemia; the lively chatter, the cigarette smoke, the interchange of bright smiles and eye-glances — all this display and magnificence overpowered the daughter of Mrs. Dempsey and held her motionless.

Mr. Brunelli stepped into the yard and seemed to spread his smile and bow over the entire company. And everywhere there was a great clapping of hands and a few cries of " Bravo ! " and " 'Tonio ! 'Tonio ! " whatever those words might mean. Ladies waved their napkins at him, gentlemen almost twisted their necks off, trying to catch his nod.

When the ovation was concluded Mr. Brunelli, with a final bow, stepped nimbly into the kitchen and flung off his coat and waistcoat.

Flaherty, the nimblest " garsong " among the waiters, had been assigned to the special service of Katy. She was a little faint from hunger, for the Irish stew on the Dempsey table had been particularly weak that day. Delicious odors from unknown dishes tantalized her. And Flaherty began to bring to her table course after course of ambrosial food that the gods might have pronounced excellent.

But even in the midst of her Lucullian repast Katy laid down her knife and fork. Her heart sank as lead, and a tear fell upon her filet mignon. Her haunting suspicions of the star lodger arose again, fourfold. Thus courted and admired and smiled upon by that fashionable and gracious assembly, what else could Mr. Brunelli be but one of those dazzling titled patricians, glorious of name but shy of rent money, concerning whom experience had made her wise? With a sense of his ineligibility growing within her there was mingled a torturing conviction that his personality was becoming more pleasing to her day by day. And why had he left her to dine alone?

But here he was coming again, now coatless, his snowy shirt-sleeves rolled high above his Jeffries-onian elbows, a white yachting cap perched upon his jetty curls.

" 'Tonio! 'Tonio!" shouted many, and " The spaghetti! The spaghetti!" shouted the rest.

Never at 'Tonio's did a waiter dare to serve a dish of spaghetti until 'Tonio came to test it, to prove the sauce and add the needful dash of seasoning that gave it perfection.

From table to table moved 'Tonio, like a prince in his palace, greeting his guests. White, jewelled hands signalled him from every side.

A glass of wine with this one and that, smiles for all, a jest and repartee for any that might challenge — truly few princes could be so agreeable a host! And what artist could ask for further appreciation of his handiwork? Katy did not know that the proudest consummation of a New Yorker's ambition is to shake hands with a spaghetti chef or to receive a nod from a Broadway head-waiter.

At last the company thinned, leaving but a few couples and quartettes lingering over new wine and old stories. And then came Mr. Brunelli to Katy's secluded table, and drew a chair close to hers.

Katy smiled at him dreamily. She was eating the last spoonful of a raspberry roll with Burgundy sauce.

"You have seen!" said Mr. Brunelli, laying one hand upon his collar bone. "I am Antonio Brunelli! Yes; I am the great 'Tonio! You have not suspect that! I loave you, Katy, and you shall marry with me. Is it not so? Call me 'Antonio,' and say that you will be mine."

Katy's head drooped to the shoulder that was now freed from all suspicion of having received the knightly accolade.

"Oh, Andy," she sighed, "this is great! Sure, I'll marry wid ye. But why didn't ye tell me ye was the cook? I was near turnin' ye down for bein' one of thim foreign counts!"

FROM EACH ACCORDING TO HIS
ABILITY

VUYNING left his club, cursing it softly, without any particular anger. From ten in the morning until eleven it had bored him immeasurably. Kirk with his fish story, Brooks with his Porto Rico cigars, old Morrison with his anecdote about the widow, Hepburn with his invariable luck at billiards — all these afflictions had been repeated without change of bill or scenery. Besides these morning evils Miss Allison had refused him again on the night before. But that was a chronic trouble. Five times she had laughed at his offer to make her Mrs. Vuyning. He intended to ask her again the next Wednesday evening.

Vuyning walked along Forty-fourth Street to Broadway, and then drifted down the great sluice that washes out the dust of the gold-mines of Gotham. He wore a morning suit of light gray, low, dull kid shoes, a plain, finely woven straw hat, and his visible linen was the most delicate possible shade of heliotrope. His necktie was the blue-gray of a November sky, and its knot was plainly the outcome of a lordly carelessness combined with an accurate conception of the most recent dictum of fashion.

Now, to write of a man's haberdashery is a worse

thing than to write a historical novel "around" Paul Jones, or to pen a testimonial to a hay-fever cure.

Therefore, let it be known that the description of Vuyning's apparel is germane to the movements of the story, and not to make room for the new fall stock of goods.

Even Broadway that morning was a discord in Vuyning's ears; and in his eyes it paralleled for a few dreamy, dreary minutes a certain howling, scorching, seething, malodorous slice of street that he remembered in Morocco. He saw the struggling mass of dogs, beggars, fakirs, slave-drivers and veiled women in carts without horses, the sun blazing brightly among the bazaars, the piles of rubbish from ruined temples in the street — and then a lady, passing, jabbed the ferrule of a parasol in his side and brought him back to Broadway.

Five minutes of his stroll brought him to a certain corner, where a number of silent, pale-faced men are accustomed to stand, immovably, for hours, busy with the file blades of their penknives, with their hat brims on a level with their eyelids. Wall Street speculators, driving home in their carriages, love to point out these men to their visiting friends and tell them of this rather famous lounging-place of the "crooks." On Wall Street the speculators never use the file blades of their knives.

Vuyning was delighted when one of this company stepped forth and addressed him as he was passing. He was hungry for something out of the ordinary, and to be accosted by this smooth-faced, keen-eyed, low-voiced, athletic member of the under world, with his grim, yet pleasant smile, had all the taste of an adventure to the convention-weary Vuyning.

" Excuse me, friend," said he. " Could I have a few minutes' talk with you — on the level? "

" Certainly," said Vuyning, with a smile. " But, suppose we step aside to a quieter place. There is a divan — a café over here that will do. Schrumm will give us a private corner."

Schrumm established them under a growing palm, with two seidls between them. Vuyning made a pleasant reference to meteorological conditions, thus forming a hinge upon which might be swung the door leading from the thought repository of the other.

" In the first place," said his companion, with the air of one who presents his credentials, " I want you to understand that I am a crook. Out West I am known as Rowdy the Dude. Pickpocket, supper man, second-story man, yeggman, boxman, all-round burglar, card-sharp and slickest con man west of the Twenty-third Street ferry landing — that's my history. That's to show I'm on the square — with you. My name's Emerson."

" Confound old Kirk with his fish stories," said Vuyning to himself, with silent glee as he went through his pockets for a card. " It's pronounced ' Vining,' " he said, as he tossed it over to the other. " And I'll be as frank with you. I'm just a kind of a loafer, I guess, living on my daddy's money. At the club they call me ' Left-at-the-Post.' I never did a day's work in my life; and I haven't the heart to run over a chicken when I'm motoring. It's a pretty shabby record, altogether."

" There's one thing you can do," said Emerson, admiringly; " you can carry duds. I've watched you several times pass on Broadway. You look the best dressed man I've seen. And I'll bet you a gold mine I've got $50 worth more gent's furnishings on my frame than you have. That's what I wanted to see you about. I can't do the trick. Take a look at me. What's wrong? "

" Stand up," said Vuyning.

Emerson arose, and slowly revolved.

" You've been ' outfitted,' " declared the clubman. " Some Broadway window-dresser has misused you. That's an expensive suit, though, Emerson."

" A hundred dollars," said Emerson.

" Twenty too much," said Vuyning. " Six months' old in cut, one inch too long, and half an inch too much lapel. Your hat is plainly dated one year ago, although there's only a sixteenth of an inch lacking

in the brim to tell the story. That English poke in
your collar is too short by the distance between Troy
and London. A plain gold link cuff-button would
take all the shine out of those pearl ones with diamond settings. Those tan shoes would be exactly
the articles to work into the heart of a Brooklyn
school-ma'am on a two weeks' visit to Lake Ronkon-
koma. I think I caught a glimpse of a blue silk
sock embroidered with russet lilies of the valley when
you — improperly — drew up your trousers as you
sat down. There are always plain ones to be had
in the stores. Have I hurt your feelings, Emerson?"

"Double the ante!" cried the criticised one, greed-
ily. "Give me more of it. There's a way to tote
the haberdashery, and I want to get wise to it. Say,
you're the right kind of a swell. Anything else to the
queer about me?"

"Your tie," said Vuyning, "is tied with absolute
precision and correctness."

"Thanks," gratefully —"I spent over half an
hour at it before I ——"

"Thereby," interrupted Vuyning, "completing
your resemblance to a dummy in a Broadway store
window."

"Yours truly," said Emerson, sitting down again.
"It's bully of you to put me wise. I knew there
was something wrong, but I couldn't just put my

finger on it. I guess it comes by nature to know how to wear clothes."

"Oh, I suppose," said Vuyning, with a laugh, "that my ancestors picked up the knack while they were peddling clothes from house to house a couple of hundred years ago. I'm told they did that."

"And mine," said Emerson, cheerfully, "were making their visits at night, I guess, and didn't have a chance to catch on to the correct styles."

"I tell you what," said Vuyning, whose ennui had taken wings, "I'll take you to my tailor. He'll eliminate the mark of the beast from your exterior. That is, if you care to go any further in the way of expense."

"Play 'em to the ceiling," said Emerson, with a boyish smile of joy. "I've got a roll as big around as a barrel of black-eyed peas and as loose as the wrapper of a two-for-fiver. I don't mind telling you that I was not touring among the Antipodes when the burglar-proof safe of the Farmers' National Bank of Butterville, Ia., flew open some moonless nights ago to the tune of $16,000."

"Aren't you afraid," asked Vuyning, "that I'll call a cop and hand you over?"

"You tell me," said Emerson, coolly, "why I didn't keep them."

He laid Vuyning's pocketbook and watch — the Vuyning 100-year-old family watch — on the table.

" Man," said Vuyning, revelling, " did you ever hear the tale Kirk tells about the six-pound trout and the old fisherman? "

" Seems not," said Emerson, politely. " I'd like to."

" But you won't," said Vuyning. " I've heard it scores of times. That's why I won't tell you. I was just thinking how much better this is than a club. Now, shall we go to my tailor? "

.   .   .   .   .

" Boys, and elderly gents," said Vuyning, five days later at his club, standing up against the window where his coterie was gathered, and keeping out the breeze, " a friend of mine from the West will dine at our table this evening."

" Will he ask if we have heard the latest from Denver? " said a member, squirming in his chair.

" Will he mention the new twenty-three-story Masonic Temple, in Quincy, Ill.? " inquired another, dropping his nose-glasses.

" Will he spring one of those Western Mississippi River catfish stories, in which they use yearling calves for bait? " demanded Kirk, fiercely.

" Be comforted," said Vuyning. " He has none of the little vices. He is a burglar and safe-blower, and a pal of mine."

" Oh, Mary Ann! " said they. " Must you always adorn every statement with your alleged humor? "

It came to pass that at eight in the evening a calm, smooth, brilliant, affable man sat at Vuyning's right hand during dinner. And when the ones who pass their lives in city streets spoke of skyscrapers or of the little Czar on his far, frozen throne, or of insignificant fish from inconsequential streams, this big, deep-chested man, faultlessly clothed, and eyed like an Emperor, disposed of their Lilliputian chatter with a wink of his eyelash.

And then he painted for them with hard, broad strokes a marvellous lingual panorama of the West. He stacked snow-topped mountains on the table, freezing the hot dishes of the waiting diners. With a wave of his hand he swept the clubhouse into a pine-crowned gorge, turning the waiters into a grim posse, and each listener into a blood-stained fugitive, climbing with torn fingers upon the ensanguined rocks. He touched the table and spake, and the five panted as they gazed on barren lava beds, and each man took his tongue between his teeth and felt his mouth bake at the tale of a land empty of water and food. As simply as Homer sang, while he dug a tine of his fork leisurely into the tablecloth, he opened a new world to their view, as does one who tells a child of the Looking-Glass Country.

As one of his listeners might have spoken of tea too strong at a Madison Square " afternoon," so he depicted the ravages of " redeye " in a border town when the caballeros of the lariat and "forty-five" reduced ennui to a minimum.

And then, with a sweep of his white, unringed hands, he dismissed Melpomene, and forthwith Diana and Amaryllis footed it before the mind's eyes of the clubmen.

The savannas of the continent spread before them. The wind, humming through a hundred leagues of sage brush and mesquite, closed their ears to the city's staccato noises. He told them of camps, of ranches marooned in a sea of fragrant prairie blossoms, of gallops in the stilly night that Apollo would have forsaken his daytime steeds to enjoy; he read them the great, rough epic of the cattle and the hills that have not been spoiled by the hand of man, the mason. His words were a telescope to the city men, whose eyes had looked upon Youngstown, O., and whose tongues had called it "West."

In fact, Emerson had them "going."

. . . . .

The next morning at ten he met Vuyning, by appointment, at a Forty-second Street café.

Emerson was to leave for the West that day. He wore a suit of dark cheviot that looked to have been draped upon him by an ancient Grecian tailor who was a few thousand years ahead of the styles.

"Mr. Vuyning," said he, with the clear, ingenuous smile of the successful "crook," "it's up to me to go the limit for you any time I can do so. You're the real thing; and if I can ever return the favor, you bet your life I'll do it."

"What was that cow-puncher's name?" asked Vuyning, "who used to catch a mustang by the nose and mane, and throw him till he put the bridle on?"

"Bates," said Emerson.

"Thanks," said Vuyning. "I thought it was Yates. Oh, about that toggery business — I'd forgotten that."

"I've been looking for some guy to put me on the right track for years," said Emerson. "You're the goods, duty free, and half-way to the warehouse in a red wagon."

"Bacon, toasted on a green willow switch over red coals, ought to put broiled lobsters out of business," said Vuyning. "And you say a horse at the end of a thirty-foot rope can't pull a ten-inch stake out of wet prairie? Well, good-bye, old man, if you must be off."

At one o'clock Vuyning had luncheon with Miss Allison by previous arrangement.

For thirty minutes he babbled to her, unaccountably, of ranches, horses, cañons, cyclones, round-ups, Rocky Mountains and beans and bacon. She looked at him with wondering and half-terrified eyes.

"I was going to propose again to-day," said Vuyning, cheerily, "but I won't. I've worried you often enough. You know dad has a ranch in Colorado. What's the good of staying here? Jumping jonquils! but it's great out there. I'm going to start next Tuesday."

"No, you won't," said Miss Allison.

"What?" said Vuyning.

"Not alone," said Miss Allison, dropping a tear upon her salad. "What do you think?"

"Betty!" exclaimed Vuyning, "what do you mean?"

"I'll go too," said Miss Allison, forcibly.

Vuyning filled her glass with Apollinaris.

"Here's to Rowdy the Dude!" he gave — a toast mysterious.

"Don't know him," said Miss Allison; "but if he's your friend, Jimmy — here goes!"

THE MEMENTO

MISS LYNNETTE D'ARMANDE turned her back on Broadway. This was but tit for tat, because Broadway had often done the same thing to Miss D'Armande. Still, the "tats" seemed to have it, for the ex-leading lady of the "Reaping the Whirlwind" company had everything to ask of Broadway, while there was no vice-versâ.

So Miss Lynnette D'Armande turned the back of her chair to her window that overlooked Broadway, and sat down to stitch in time the lisle-thread heel of a black silk stocking. The tumult and glitter of the roaring Broadway beneath her window had no charm for her; what she greatly desired was the stifling air of a dressing-room on that fairyland street and the roar of an audience gathered in that capricious quarter. In the meantime, those stockings must not be neglected. Silk does wear out so, but — after all, isn't it just the only goods there is?

The Hotel Thalia looks on Broadway as Marathon looks on the sea. It stands like a gloomy cliff above the whirlpool where the tides of two great thoroughfares clash. Here the player-bands gather at the end of their wanderings, to loosen the buskin and dust the sock. Thick in the streets around it are booking-

offices, theatres, agents, schools, and the lobster-pal-
aces to which those thorny paths lead.

Wandering through the eccentric halls of the dim
and fusty Thalia, you seem to have found yourself
in some great ark or caravan about to sail, or fly, or
roll away on wheels. About the house lingers a sense
of unrest, of expectation, of transientness, even of
anxiety and apprehension. The halls are a labyrinth.
Without a guide, you wander like a lost soul in a
Sam Loyd puzzle.

Turning any corner, a dressing-sack or a *cul-de-sac*
may bring you up short. You meet alarming
tragedians stalking in bath-robes in search of ru-
mored bathrooms. From hundreds of rooms come the
buzz of talk, scraps of new and old songs, and the
ready laughter of the convened players.

Summer has come; their companies have disbanded,
and they take their rest in their favorite caravansary,
while they besiege the managers for engagements for
the coming season.

At this hour of the afternoon the day's work of
tramping the rounds of the agents' offices is over.
Past you, as you ramble distractedly through the
mossy halls, flit audible visions of houris, with veiled,
starry eyes, flying tag-ends of things and a swish of
silk, bequeathing to the dull hallways an odor of
gaiety and a memory of *frangipanni*. Serious young
comedians, with versatile Adam's apples, gather in

doorways and talk of Booth. Far-reaching from
somewhere comes the smell of ham and red cabbage,
and the crash of dishes on the American plan.

The indeterminate hum of life in the Thalia is
enlivened by the discreet popping — at reasonable
and salubrious intervals — of beer-bottle corks.
Thus punctuated, life in the genial hostel scans easily
— the comma being the favorite mark, semicolons
frowned upon, and periods barred.

Miss D'Armande's room was a small one. There
was room for her rocker between the dresser and the
wash-stand if it were placed longitudinally. On the
dresser were its usual accoutrements, plus the ex-leading lady's collected souvenirs of road engagements
and photographs of her dearest and best professional
friends.

At one of these photographs she looked twice or
thrice as she darned, and smiled friendlily.

" I'd like to know where Lee is just this minute,"
she said, half-aloud.

If you had been privileged to view the photograph
thus flattered, you would have thought at the first
glance that you saw the picture of a many-petalled
white flower, blown through the air by a storm. But
the floral kingdom was not responsible for that swirl
of petalous whiteness.

You saw the filmy, brief skirt of Miss Rosalie Ray
as she made a complete heels-over-head turn in her

wistaria-entwined swing, far out from the stage, high above the heads of the audience. You saw the camera's inadequate representation of the graceful, strong kick, with which she, at this exciting moment, sent flying, high and far, the yellow silk garter that each evening spun from her agile limb and descended upon the delighted audience below.

You saw, too, amid the black-clothed, mainly masculine patrons of select vaudeville a hundred hands raised with the hope of staying the flight of the brilliant aërial token.

Forty weeks of the best circuits this act had brought Miss Rosalie Ray, for each of two years. She did other things during her twelve minutes — a song and dance, imitations of two or three actors who are but imitations of themselves, and a balancing feat with a step-ladder and feather-duster; but when the blossom-decked swing was let down from the flies, and Miss Rosalie sprang smiling into the seat, with the golden circlet conspicuous in the place whence it was soon to slide and become a soaring and coveted guerdon — then it was that the audience rose in its seat as a single man — or presumably so — and indorsed the specialty that made Miss Ray's name a favorite in the booking-offices.

At the end of the two years Miss Ray suddenly announced to her dear friend, Miss D'Armande, that she was going to spend the summer at an antediluvian village on the north shore of Long Island, and that the stage would see her no more.

Seventeen minutes after Miss Lynnette D'Armande had expressed her wish to know the whereabouts of her old chum, there were sharp raps at her door.

Doubt not that it was Rosalie Ray. At the shrill command to enter she did so, with something of a tired flutter, and dropped a heavy hand-bag on the floor. Upon my word, it was Rosalie, in a loose, travel-stained automobileless coat, closely tied brown veil with yard-long, flying ends, gray walking-suit and tan oxfords with lavender overgaiters.

When she threw off her veil and hat, you saw a pretty enough face, now flushed and disturbed by some unusual emotion, and restless, large eyes with discontent marring their brightness. A heavy pile of dull auburn hair, hastily put up, was escaping in crinkly, waving strands and curling, small locks from the confining combs and pins.

The meeting of the two was not marked by the effusion vocal, gymnastical, osculatory and catechetical that distinguishes the greetings of their unprofessional sisters in society. There was a brief clinch, two simultaneous labial dabs and they stood on the same footing of the old days. Very much like the short salutations of soldiers or of travellers in foreign wilds are the welcomes between the strollers at the corners of their criss-cross roads.

"I've got the hall-room two flights up above yours," said Rosalie, "but I came straight to see you before going up. I didn't know you were here till they told me."

"I've been in since the last of April," said Lynnette. "And I'm going on the road with a 'Fatal Inheritance' company. We open next week in Elizabeth. I thought you'd quit the stage, Lee. Tell me about yourself."

Rosalie settled herself with a skilful wriggle on the top of Miss D'Armande's wardrobe trunk, and leaned her head against the papered wall. From long habit, thus can peripatetic leading ladies and their sisters make themselves as comfortable as though the deepest armchairs embraced them.

"I'm going to tell you, Lynn," she said, with a strangely sardonic and yet carelessly resigned look on her youthful face. "And then to-morrow I'll strike the old Broadway trail again, and wear some more paint off the chairs in the agents' offices. If anybody had told me any time in the last three months up to four o'clock this afternoon that I'd ever listen to that 'Leave-your-name-and-address' rot of the booking bunch again, I'd have given 'em the real Mrs. Fiske laugh. Loan me a handkerchief, Lynn. Gee! but those Long Island trains are fierce. I've got enough soft-coal cinders on my face to go on and play

Topsy without using the cork. And, speaking of corks — got anything to drink, Lynn? "

Miss D'Armande opened a door of the wash-stand and took out a bottle.

" There's nearly a pint of Manhattan. There's a cluster of carnations in the drinking glass, but ——"

" Oh, pass the bottle. Save the glass for company. Thanks! That hits the spot. The same to you. My first drink in three months!

" Yes, Lynn, I quit the stage at the end of last season. I quit it because I was sick of the life. And especially because my heart and soul were sick of men — of the kind of men we stage people have to be up against. You know what the game is to us — it's a fight against 'em all the way down the line from the manager who wants us to try his new motor-car to the bill-posters who want to call us by our front names.

" And the men we have to meet after the show are the worst of all. The stage-door kind, and the manager's friends who take us to supper and show their diamonds and talk about seeing ' Dan ' and ' Dave ' and ' Charlie ' for us. They're beasts, and I hate 'em.

" I tell you, Lynn, it's the girls like us on the stage that ought to be pitied. It's girls from good homes that are honestly ambitious and work hard to rise in the profession, but never do get there. You hear a lot of sympathy sloshed around on chorus girls and their fifteen dollars a week. Piffle! There ain't a sorrow in the chorus that a lobster cannot heal.

"If there's any tears to shed, let 'em fall for the actress that gets a salary of from thirty to forty-five dollars a week for taking a leading part in a bum show. She knows she'll never do any better; but she hangs on for years, hoping for the 'chance' that never comes.

"And the fool plays we have to work in! Having another girl roll you around the stage by the hind legs in a 'Wheelbarrow Chorus' in a musical comedy is dignified drama compared with the idiotic things I've had to do in the thirty-centers.

"But what I hated most was the men — the men leering and blathering at you across tables, trying to buy you with Würzburger or Extra Dry, according to their estimate of your price. And the men in the audiences, clapping, yelling, snarling, crowding, writhing, gloating — like a lot of wild beasts, with their eyes fixed on you, ready to eat you up if you come in reach of their claws. Oh, how I hate 'em!

"Well, I'm not telling you much about myself, am I, Lynn?

"I had two hundred dollars saved up, and I cut the stage the first of the summer. I went over on Long Island and found the sweetest little village that ever was, called Soundport, right on the water. I was going to spend the summer there, and study up on elocution, and try to get a class in the fall. There was an old widow lady with a cottage near the beach who sometimes rented a room or two just for company, and she took me in. She had another boarder, too — the Reverend Arthur Lyle.

" Yes, he was the head-liner. You're on, Lynn. I'll tell you all of it in a minute. It's only a one-act play.

" The first time he walked on, Lynn, I felt myself going; the first lines he spoke, he had me. He was different from the men in audiences. He was tall and slim, and you never heard him come in the room, but you *felt* him. He had a face like a picture of a knight — like one of that Round Table bunch — and a voice like a 'cello solo. And his manners!

" Lynn, if you'd take John Drew in his best drawing-room scene and compare the two, you'd have John arrested for disturbing the peace.

" I'll spare you the particulars; but in less than a month Arthur and I were engaged. He preached at a little one-night stand of a Methodist church. There was to be a parsonage the size of a lunch-wagon, and hens and honeysuckles when we were married. Arthur used to preach to me a good deal about Heaven, but he never could get my mind quite off those honeysuckles and hens.

" No; I didn't tell him I'd been on the stage. I hated the business and all that went with it; I'd cut it out forever, and I didn't see any use of stirring

things up. I was a good girl, and I didn't have anything to confess, except being an elocutionist, and
that was about all the strain my conscience would
stand.

"Oh, I tell you, Lynn, I was happy. I sang in
the choir and attended the sewing society, and re-
cited that ' Annie Laurie ' thing with the whistling
stunt in it, ' in a manner bordering upon the professional,' as the weekly village paper reported it. And
Arthur and I went rowing, and walking in the woods,
and clamming, and that poky little village seemed to
me the best place in the world. I'd have been happy
to live there always, too, if ——

"But one morning old Mrs. Gurley, the widow
lady, got gossipy while I was helping her string beans
on the back porch, and began to gush information, as
folks who rent out their rooms usually do. Mr. Lyle
was her idea of a saint on earth — as he was mine,
too. She went over all his virtues and graces, and
wound up by telling me that Arthur had had an ex-
tremely romantic love-affair, not long before, that had
ended unhappily. She didn't seem to be on to the details, but she knew that he had been hit pretty hard.
He was paler and thinner, she said, and he had some
kind of a remembrance or keepsake of the lady in a
little rosewood box that he kept locked in his desk
drawer in his study.

" ' Several times,' says she, ' I've seen him

gloomerin' over that box of evenings, and he always
locks it up right away if anybody comes into the
room.'

"Well, you can imagine how long it was before I
got Arthur by the wrist and led him down stage and
hissed in his ear.

"That same afternoon we were lazying around in a
boat among the water-lilies at the edge of the bay.

"'Arthur,' says I, 'you never told me you'd had
another love-affair. But Mrs. Gurley did,' I went on,
to let him know I knew. I hate to hear a man lie.

"'Before you came,' says he, looking me frankly
in the eye, 'there was a previous affection — a strong
one. Since you know of it, I will be perfectly candid
with you.'

"'I am waiting,' says I.

"'My dear Ida,' says Arthur — of course I went
by my real name, while I was in Soundport —'this
former affection was a spiritual one, in fact. Although the lady aroused my deepest sentiments, and
was, as I thought, my ideal woman, I never met her,
and never spoke to her. It was an ideal love. My
love for you, while no less ideal, is different. You
wouldn't let that come between us.'

"'Was she pretty?' I asked.

"'She was very beautiful,' said Arthur.

"'Did you see her often?' I asked.

"'Something like a dozen times,' says he.

"'Always from a distance?' says I.

"'Always from quite a distance,' says he.

"'And you loved her?' I asked.

"'She seemed my ideal of beauty and grace — and soul,' says Arthur.

"'And this keepsake that you keep under lock and key, and moon over at times, is that a remembrance from her?'

"'A memento,' says Arthur, 'that I have treasured.'

"'Did she send it to you?'

"'It came to me from her,' says he.

"'In a roundabout way?' I asked.

"'Somewhat roundabout,' says he, 'and yet rather direct.'

"'Why didn't you ever meet her?' I asked. 'Were your positions in life so different?'

"'She was far above me,' says Arthur. 'Now, Ida,' he goes on, 'this is all of the past. You're not going to be jealous, are you?'

"'Jealous!' says I. 'Why, man, what are you talking about? It makes me think ten times as much of you as I did before I knew about it.'

"And it did, Lynn — if you can understand it. That ideal love was a new one on me, but it struck me as being the most beautiful and glorious thing I'd ever heard of. Think of a man loving a woman he'd never even spoken to, and being faithful just to what his mind and heart pictured her! Oh, it sounded great to me. The men I'd always known come at you with either diamonds, knock-out-drops or a raise of salary,— and their ideals!— well, we'll say no more.

"Yes, it made me think more of Arthur than I did before. I couldn't be jealous of that far-away divinity that he used to worship, for I was going to have him myself. And I began to look upon him as a saint on earth, just as old lady Gurley did.

"About four o'clock this afternoon a man came to the house for Arthur to go and see somebody that was sick among his church bunch. Old lady Gurley was taking her afternoon snore on a couch, so that left me pretty much alone.

"In passing by Arthur's study I looked in, and saw his bunch of keys hanging in the drawer of his desk, where he'd forgotten 'em. Well, I guess we're all to the Mrs. Bluebeard now and then, ain't we, Lynn? I made up my mind I'd have a look at that memento he kept so secret. Not that I cared what it was — it was just curiosity.

"While I was opening the drawer I imagined one or two things it might be. I thought it might be a dried rosebud she'd dropped down to him from a balcony, or maybe a picture of her he'd cut out of a magazine, she being so high up in the world.

" I opened the drawer, and there was the rosewood casket about the size of a gent's collar box. I found the little key in the bunch that fitted it, and unlocked it and raised the lid.

" I took one look at that memento, and then I went to my room and packed my trunk. I threw a few things into my grip, gave my hair a flirt or two with a side-comb, put on my hat, and went in and gave the old lady's foot a kick. I'd tried awfully hard to use proper and correct language while I was there for Arthur's sake, and I had the habit down pat, but it left me then.

" ' Stop sawing gourds,' says I, ' and sit up and take notice. The ghost's about to walk. I'm going away from here, and I owe you eight dollars. The expressman will call for my trunk.'

" I handed her the money.

" ' Dear me, Miss Crosby!' says she. ' Is anything wrong? I thought you were pleased here. Dear me, young women are so hard to understand, and so different from what you expect 'em to be.'

" ' You're damn right,' says I. ' Some of 'em are. But you can't say that about men. *When you know one man you know 'em all!* That settles the human-race question.'

" And then I caught the four-thirty-eight, soft-coal unlimited; and here I am."

" You didn't tell me what was in the box, Lee," said Miss D'Armande, anxiously.

"One of those yellow silk garters that I used to kick off my leg into the audience during that old vaudeville swing act of mine. Is there any of the cocktail left, Lynn? "

THE END

THE COUNTRY LIFE PRESS
GARDEN CITY, N. Y.